Astrocytoma

Astrocytoma

My Journey

Meredith Joy Merritt

Library Partners Press

Winston-Salem, NC

This memoir is nonfiction. Some names and identifying details have been changed to protect the privacy of the people involved.

Cover design: Celeste Holcomb

Front Cover art:

Foreground collage: "Rain of Stars," by Meredith Joy Merritt

Background field: "Pink Tectonics," by Meredith Joy Merritt

Back cover photo by Donald Beagle, 2019

ISBN 978-1-61846-123-0

Produced and Distributed By:

Library Partners Press

ZSR Library

Wake Forest University

1834 Wake Forest Road

Winston-Salem, North Carolina 27106

www.librarypartnerspress.org

Manufactured in the United States of America

Contents

DEDICATION   xi

ACKNOWLEDGEMENT   xiii

PART ONE   *1*

THE TULIP   *3*

THE LEARNING CURVE   *7*

THE FLOOD   *11*

SALEM IS WATCHING THE SWIFTLY FLYING   *13*

SCIENCE IS KING   *15*

THE MONK IS HUNGRY   *19*

MAPPA MUNDI   *23*

SHORT WORK   *25*

AN ANGELIC VISITATION   *27*

THE DAY BEFORE THE DAY BEFORE   *29*

POP!   *31*

THE DAY ARRIVES   *35*

PART TWO   *39*

EMERGING   *41*

WHAT KIND OF ANIMAL?   *43*

POOR PHIL GREEN   *47*

DEPARTURES   *49*

PART THREE   *53*

THE WRONG PANTS   *55*

MY PILLS ARE MESSED UP   *57*

WHERE IS LUCY?   *59*

TRANSPORT   *61*

ONCOLOGY   *63*

ALIEN   *67*

HAZARDOUS MATERIALS   *69*

DYSARTHRIA   *71*

PART FOUR   *73*

BOMB   *75*

A TOUR OF EGYPT   *77*

POISON   *81*

WONDROUS LOVE   *83*

THIS IS NOT MY ROOM   *85*

THE SEAMSTRESS   *89*

WHERE IS THAT WORD?   *93*

CATS ON THE RUN   *95*

PUZZLES   *97*

SISTERS   *99*

NUMBER HASH   *101*

CONTESTED NOODLES   *105*

CABBAGE HEAD   *107*

PROGRESS   *109*

THE CLOUD OF UNKNOWING   *111*

THE SHOALS   *113*

PART FIVE   *115*

I DIDN'T MEAN TO SAY THAT   *117*

KWANZAN MOVING FLOWERS   *119*

CAT TOOTH FOOD   *121*

HEISENBERG AT THE TABLE   *123*

NICER   *125*

PART SIX   *127*

THE VALLEY   *129*

ANIMAL LOVERS FOREVER   *131*

SILENT TEARS   *133*

STANLEY YATES MERRITT 1926–2019   *135*

NOT YOU   *139*

MY RABBIT   *141*

PEAKS OF OTTER	*143*
WELCOME TO THE DUST BIN	*145*
SENESCENCE	*147*
FALLING STAR	*149*
DOWN-A-DAY A-DOWN A-HEY	*151*
MIDNIGHT BEAK	*153*
REPEAT AFTER ME	*155*
FUNERALS	*157*
PART SEVEN	*159*
BOY COY TOY	*161*
DARK SHADOWS	*163*
IT'S ALL IN YOUR HEAD	*165*
PRAISE FOR THE FISH	*167*
NEW POTATOES	*171*
A WASTED AFTERNOON	*175*
LOSING THE TIMELESS	*179*
THERAVADAN	*181*
PEMA TARA	*185*
TIME'S ARROW	*189*
GOODBY AND HELLO	*191*
PART EIGHT	*195*
IT'S FINALLY TIME	*197*

SPOONS   *201*

GAMES   *203*

STORIES   *205*

BELMONT ABBEY   *209*

SENTENCE BUILDING   *213*

RUBY'S QUEST   *215*

NON-DUALISTIC EXPERIENCE   *219*

END OF SPEECH THERAPY   *221*

EPILOGUE   *223*
THE JUGGLER   *225*

DEDICATION

I dedicate this book to Donald Robert Beagle

My true love and helpmeet

ACKNOWLEDGEMENT

To Hans Christian von Baeyer,
My teacher

PART ONE

TERRA INCOGNITA

THE TULIP

There is something seriously wrong with the coffee maker. The coffee is dripping into the plate where the carafe is supposed to sit. I forgot to put the carafe in. Silly. I start over.

Now it's the laundry. I move the clothes into the dryer and set the timer, but press the button to start the washer instead of pressing the knob to turn the dryer on.

Poor attention, I think, probably related to Multiple Sclerosis. MS has played tricks on my brain before and I wonder if I should call Dr. Johnson, my neurologist. He will probably tell me to take steroids, which make me monstrously fat and I'm vain. Maybe I should just be extra careful with machines from now on; nothing serious really has happened. I have a regular appointment in a couple of weeks and I plan to talk with him about it then.

Two weeks pass and I go to my scheduled check-in with Dr. Johnson, where I say "Look, I've had some lapses in attention," not elaborating. I've become an expert on second-guessing doctors since I retired on disability, specifying when I think no medication is needed.

"Oh, don't worry, people with MS have problems with atten-

3

tion all the time," he says, waving his hand as if to banish my worry.

So, I think, I'll leave it at that, never mind the fine print.

I have a writing project going on and am finding it slow. "The family plays" I write, when I mean to say they "played." Errors in verb tenses seem to have cropped up a lot lately, along with a variety of other grammatical lapses and mis-spellings, and one day it takes me an hour to finish a page. This is highly unusual for me, having been a tenured Associate Professor at UNC-Charlotte, churning out papers at a brisk pace.

I think about the coffee machine and the laundry and admit that something is going on and realize that I've been foolish. Steroids or not, I call Dr. Johnson's office and say that I need a new MRI, the abbreviation for an examination using "Magnetic Resonance Imaging."

This is not an X-ray but rather uses magnetic fields and radio waves to generate detailed pictures of organs within the body. Brain MRI's are one of the best ways for a neurologist to get an idea what's happening with MS patients, since the disease manifests in the central nervous system.

"Yes, he says you can have a new one," Joyce, Dr. Johnson's nurse, informs me when she calls back. "It's time for you to have one anyway."

Dutifully, I report to the hospital and get into the tube that is used to slide the patient under the magnetic coil. I, unlike many people, don't feel claustrophobic inside. MRI machines make a lot of noise, which most people detest, but I actually like it. To me, it sounds like ultra-modern music with unusual percussion. You have a lot of MRIs with MS, and I am familiar enough with them that I don't feel worried, just annoyed that I might have a new lesion.

The next morning, Friday, Joyce, Dr. Johnson's nurse, calls.

"Dr. Johnson said to get over here. Immediately!" she says, and the tone of her voice tells me she is frightened.

Baffled, Don, my husband drops his plans to go to work and we jump in the car, driving straight to the office, twenty minutes to Huntersville, not talking. Dr. Johnson is waiting with MRI films clipped above his desk. "Sit down, I have bad news," he advises.

Glaring out of the film is a white image in the upper left side of my head that looks like a misshapen tulip, with three petals.

"You have a brain tumor," Dr. Johnson announces. "You have a glioma. There are several types of glioma, but we won't know those specifics until the surgery. It could be an astrocytoma, which recently has become more treatable."

How strange to be sitting there hoping for a particular kind of brain tumor!

THE LEARNING CURVE

I have an appointment this morning with a neurosurgeon, George Andrews. Dr. Johnson has set this up so quickly that we only had to stew over the weekend.

The waiting room of Spine and Neurosurgery is full, packed with other anxious-looking people. Finally, after what feels like hours, we are called back, processed by a nurse, and left to wait a little longer. The MRI films are prominently displayed, and a blown-up image of the obscene three-lobed tulip stands out.

What will the neurosurgeon say when he arrives? "Hi, I'm Dr. Andrews, I'm going to carve up your brain?"

The door opens and a small, wiry, energetic-looking man comes in, accompanied by three other people.

"I'm Dr. Andrews," he says, in a soft Southern voice, extending his hand to Don and then to me. "This is John, my PA, Pamela, my nurse, and Ruth, our Navigator."

I am not sure what a "Navigator" is, but this doesn't seem to be right time to interrupt.

"Dr. Johnson is quite concerned about you," he observes. "We'll do everything we can to help you."

"Your tumor is in your left temporal lobe," he continues. "This

7

is, unfortunately, the part of the brain which governs language. I can remove the tumor, but you have to be aware that you may lose the ability to speak. In any case, your recovery may be quite slow."

So this is why my grammar is so messed up. I am not exactly surprised by the connection with language, but my heart sinks with the suggestion that something that drastic could happen.

"Is it malignant?" I ask.

"Probably. We'll have to biopsy it. If it is, we can do resection, radiation and chemotherapy."

Just like that, he lays out the dreaded three, cutting, burning, and poisoning, things that happen to other people, which before now could not possibly happen to me.

The "Navigator," Ruth, speaks up. "I'll be guiding you through the process," she explains. "I'll arrange for surgery and the MRI's leading up to it, and I'll be following your case throughout into post-op and your release from the hospital."

"How many MRI's?" Don asks, phone calendar out.

"Two, one to measure functional impairment, and one to make a map for Dr. Andrews to use during the surgery." she says. "Keep your phone out, we'll be going to scheduling next.

"The next time I'll see you is the day of the operation," Dr. Andrews says, rising.

We stand up too. The interview is over, a few moments to outline something that could turn out to entail months of recovery and may result in my being mute. There is nothing more to say, and we follow Ruth to a desk with someone pecking on a screen.

Christmas falls in a few weeks, so the date for surgery is set up for December 28th. The MRI's are added to the calendar, making the month look full.

This is their routine, so cut and dried, so factual. Every day they do this, deal with people whose lives are being blown to pieces. How do they manage? They seem so calm, doing their jobs, so serenely and competently.

Do they have nightmares?

THE FLOOD

My tooth hurts and Dr. Costa is poking around my mouth.

"Well, you might need a root canal," she says. "You need an antibiotic to take care of the infection. But I do have to talk to your surgeon to see if it's safe for you to take it."

"The surgery is coming up, and I might have to wait for crowns."

She shakes her head. "The antibiotic could stay in your system for a month."

I see her in the hallway, a phone glued to her ear, waiting, waiting.

"Oh, okay. That's good. Goodbye." Dr. Costa turns to me and says, "I spoke with Dr. Andrews' nurse, Julie. She says it's ok if you need to take it."

During this conversation tears have trickled between my lashes, having nothing to do with teeth, and now they are running down my cheeks.

They all come to me, the dentist, the hygienist, the receptionist. I'm weeping inconsolably, with racking sobs. They take me to the waiting room and call Don.

"Would you like some water?" someone asks. No, no, it

wouldn't help. Why do people always offer water to someone who is upset?

Fresh tears keep gushing forth. I can't hold them back.

Dr. Costa hugs me tightly. I am now gasping like a fish out of water.

Someone in the lobby looks at us, then averts his gaze.

Don comes in and folds me into his arms. Finally, I begin to calm down, but am unable to get the tears to stop.

"Thank you so much," he says. "She's worried about her brain tumor."

"We know," Dr. Costa replies. "We understand."

She hands Don the slip with the antibiotic prescription and he pockets it.

We leave, Don's arm around me, my tears still flowing down. The world is ending. My world is ending.

SALEM IS WATCHING THE SWIFTLY FLYING

We have a new coffee maker, a Moccamaster, which is supposed to be the best of the line, and we have just received a bag of Caribou Light Roast from Amazon.

The machine is not like any others I've seen; it has a water reservoir on the left, a horizontal drip, and the glass carafe on the right. It seems unlikely until I think of Bernoulli's law, which says that water seeks its own level no matter how odd the path may be.

We watch the water traversing the path to the carafe as the tantalizing smell of java fills the kitchen. We pour the coffee into our matching red and black "Biscuits and Bach" mugs, so named for a regular program on our WDAV classical radio station and sent to us as a perk for signing up for pledging a monthly donation.

As we savor the coffee in the parlor, I see that Salem, who has been sitting on the window sill, is swiveling her head back and forth rapidly as she watches a flock of birds which are furiously flying left, right, left...

"Salem is watching the quickly birds," I observe.

"What did you say?" Don asks. "Do you mean 'Salem is watching the quickly flying birds?'"

"That's what I said."

"No, you said…"

Suddenly I realize how I've botched the sentence.

This is the work of the thing growing in my head. Surgery cannot come soon enough.

SCIENCE IS KING

Levine Cancer Institute, says the sign. The sidewalks are crowded, people everywhere and cars coming and going. So many people who have cancer, and I am probably one of them. Levine Cancer Institute, I repeat to myself. That's where I really am, for a functional MRI which will show the actual malfunctions in my brain.

We drive up to the parking deck and walk to the building where imaging is done. Again, I'm astonished at how many people are milling around inside. This is not a solitary fate.

There are several desks open and we take our place in front of one. Appointment confirmed, insurance card taken, clipboard handed up. Sit over there and fill the papers out. Wait.

"Ms. Merritt?" I hear. "Over here."

I rise obediently and follow the nurse, Louise, who hands me a paper gown and invites me into a changing room.

"I have an IV port," I explain. "I need you to use it for the contrast dye."

Due to the number of MRI's and IV MS medications I've had, my veins are shredded and I have had to have a device installed in my right upper chest for anything requiring access to a vein. It's

15

called a "port." Once I was stuck 25 times to get a vein for MRI contrast dye, so I find life with the port much easier now.

"The person who does that is on break now. Do you think we can use your hand?" Louise asks.

Accessing a port is a careful art, requiring a special process and training. I need to be politic, since I will probably get to know her well. I don't want to exactly say "You can't do it."

"Hard stick" is nurse-talk for someone who is difficult to draw blood from.

"I'm the world's worst hard stick," I explain. "Nobody can get a vein on me even if they try several times. It'll be easier for you guys to use the port. I'll gladly wait until they get back."

Louise is fine about it and I sit in my gown only 15 minutes. The person who comes to do it, Maggie, is actually the one I will get to know well. As she performs the sterile puncture procedure, I ask the usual questions. Are you from Charlotte? Do you have children? Do you have pets? Maggie likes football and follows Charlotte's Carolina Panthers.

MRI chambers make a unique sound, something like "WHOOSHA WHOOSA WHOOSHA," like a giant beating heart, nothing like anything else I've ever heard. There is something rather soothing about it, as if you are being sheltered by a giant tame beast.

I am placed on the cot that is to be slid into the machine, given earplugs and a pillow under my knees, a familiar and almost ritualized routine.

The technician comes over to me, placing the tubes for the iodine dye.

"This is a functional MRI, to show areas compromised by the tumor," she explains. "I'll put a screen up with diagrams and sen-

16

tences for you to read and you think the answers to fill in the blanks."

"I don't say them?" I ask.

"No, the machine will be able to record your thought processes using measurements of cerebral blood flow with resolution to the level of neurons."

"How can it do that if I don't say something?"

"It just does, all I have to do is drop a series of screens with words for you to identify. You don't have to speak the words; you just frame them in your mind."

The first word I identify is dog. Easy.

The second word I see is...space...um, boat?

The technician says, "No, that's wrong."

I think surely I'll get the next one right. It looks to me like a book.

She says "Again, sorry, that one is wrong, too."

I feel like something is slipping through my mind each time. If it had a sound, it would sound like noodles.

Despite the disturbing misidentifications, I am overwhelmed by the beauty of this machine. What a marvel! Science is king.

THE MONK IS HUNGRY

I belong to a sangha, a group of Buddhist people who gather to meditate and receive teaching. Our head is a rare female monk. Most Theravadan female clerics are nuns, but Ayya Medhavi has taken on higher training to qualify as a monk.

Higher learning or not, Ayya is still subject to the Buddha's rule that monks are to eat donated food from their alms bowls at sunrise and noon, forgoing any later meals. Instead, people bring the food to the monks. This is called "dana," Pali from the Sanskrit root word for "donation."

I have been the manager of Ayya's dana for a couple of years, calling friends of the sangha regularly asking them what dates they wanted to bring food, building a monthly calendar. This requires continuous persistence and diplomacy. Ayya says my work on this is better than that done by anyone who has preceded me.

And now I have to tell her that I'm quitting.

"Can we talk after we're done?" I ask Ayya as I am going into the sangha's Saturday afternoon meeting.

"We're a minute early," she replies. "How about now?"

"No, we may have to talk about for a while," I tell her. She

19

looks worried but goes into the meditation room and sets up. I usually chit-chat but am quiet today.

We sit for half an hour, have a tea break, listen to a teaching, and discuss it for a while. I wonder if I should tell the other people now but am not ready to talk about with them yet. It might end in a scene like the one in the dentist's office.

The lesson is about the Four Noble Truths which gives us ways to overcome suffering. This teaching is given often, but it is especially apropos today.

After the lesson, I decide it's time for me to tell the group.

"I won't be here for a while," I explain. "I have a brain tumor and need surgery."

The shock registers, and as people leave they say "I'm sorry," "Good luck," and "I'll be thinking of you." There is nothing more for anyone to say.

After everyone has left, I say "Ayya, you need to find a new dana manager."

Shocked silence. Then "Is it malignant?"

"We think it is. It may take my ability to speak."

Trained in acceptance, she says, "Okay. This is a good challenge for you. You have a chance to follow the Four Noble Truths and confront suffering, just as we were saying."

"Am I up to it?" I wonder.

"I think you are," she reassures me. "It was my own cancer that brought me to Buddhism."

She had lymphoblastic lymphoma some years ago and survived years of agonizing treatment, including a companion who went through so much with her that he couldn't stay. That was the beginning of her quest for ordination.

"There is something I have to say," she offers with a sly grin.

"Oh, no, please don't say it…"

"Silence may be good for your meditation!"

We look at each other and start to giggle. We guffaw. We laugh for several minutes, rolling around as if this is the funniest thing we've heard.

MAPPA MUNDI

I enter the MRI chamber with trepidation this time, and the technician greets me.

"You know this MRI is going to provide a detailed map of the area of your tumor so Dr. Andrews has an exact idea of where to cut," he explains.

"Yes, that's right, he told me," I say, wanting to sound well-informed. I think of Renaissance maps showing routes for ocean voyages, one of which notes "Here be dragons" at the edge of unexplored waters. I know that we are entering unknown places, and I'm glad I like dragons so well.

"Keep perfectly still," the technician instructs as he gets me into position and slides me into the machine, and the sounds begin.

Tap tap tap tap softly on the left ear. TAP TAP TAP loud on the right. Repeat. Pulses cross my forehead. A cacophony crawls through the base of my skull. Sudden BLAST, a klaxon, right side, going on forever.

"You moved once," the technician groans,"so I have to retake a section." It must be slight, though, because it only takes a minute to make the correction.

As I slide down, he remarks "You know, you have an MS lesion scar which is also in your temporal lobe."

"Yes, of I'm aware of it; Dr. Johnson reminded me. It knocked out my ability to read, so that I just saw a jumble of words on a page, and I had to spend a year learning how to do it. I followed Chomsky's descriptions of how children learned language, started with baby books with only a noun and a subject, and worked up."

"You know," he observes, "Chomsky isn't fashionable."

I try not to snort. "Well, his process worked perfectly for me."

"I'm just saying, it may complicate your surgery, so you may lose some reading ability."

Is he supposed to giving me medical advice? Could he be right?

Deep down, I know that he has a point, and have a sinking feeling that I may not only have trouble speaking but not return to my greatest pastime.

I try to stifle the additional fear, and bluff. It's going to be fine, perfectly fine, I reassure myself but with little result. If I am honest with myself, I am scared half to death.

SHORT WORK

There are a few people I haven't told yet, probably the most important.

My list of phone contacts is on the couch next to me, but I sit looking at it for a long time before doing anything. Maybe I should start with my father and get it over with; he has multiple myeloma, a blood cancer, and I hate to add to his troubles, but he needs to know.

"Hey, Dad, how are you?"

"Oh, hey, Meredith. I'm glad to hear from you. Things have been rough—maybe you can cheer me up. My chemo stopped working and I've had to switch to a new one, which makes me feel weak. It's slowing me down on my work."

At 93, he is collecting his papers on power engineering. He has been active in IEEE for decades, well known for his work on power supplies for paper mills. In addition to delivering conference papers, he has been a consultant for many companies whose electronic machinery is old, because nobody new knows how to make repairs and modifications.

When he winds down, I say, "Look, I'm really sorry, but I have to tell you something bad. I have a brain tumor."

Long pause. Then, "is it cancer?"

"Almost certainly. The surgeon will biopsy it but he's pretty sure it is."

"Then we're in the same boat," he observes.

"Pretty much. Why don't we call often and call ourselves 'The Cancer Pals'" I joke.

"Deal," agrees.

Ellie is next. I usually tell her everything, but I haven't faced up to this.

"When did you find out about this?" she asks, shock registering in her tone of voice."

"Um, a few weeks ago."

"And you didn't tell me? Why not?"

"I just didn't know how," I try to explain. I can tell her feelings are hurt.

She sighs. "Okay. We'll come and see you as soon as you're able to have visitors."

I haven't told Anna Jo, the Unitarian minister, yet, and I hesitate. Once she knows, everyone will know.

She, too, sighs, deeply, when I break the news, and pauses, taking it in.

At last, she asks "What can we do to help? You'll need help, Don will need help. We'll take you to appointments, bring you food, whatever. I'll let the Care Team know and we'll talk."

"Thanks, Anna Jo. That's great."

Another long pause.

"I don't know what to say. I'm just so sorry," she laments.

"Yeah, me too. Me too."

It seems like hours have passed. I look at my watch and see that this all this has happened in twenty minutes.

AN ANGELIC VISITATION

Christmas dinner is with our friend Cindy, who is a docent at the Bechtler Museum of Modern Art. Her townhouse looks like a museum itself, with paintings and small sculptures in every room. I see that she has a new painting, a shamanic figure with a woman with an owl's face.

"You have a Joan Fowler. When did you get it?" I ask.

"At last month's Gallery Crawl," she replies.

Gallery Crawl happens every first Friday and you can see every gallery in NODA (standing for North Davidson Street Arts). We always go, having a fish taco on the corner and visiting all the galleries.

"This is really beautiful. I love her work. Where is Lucinda?" I ask.

A spaniel with huge, dark eyes, hears me and comes up to give me a lick.

I notice that there are some people I don't know. Cindy introduces me to them and I begin a conversation with a striking woman named Linda.

"I've just gotten back from England," she says and we talk about my junior year abroad at Exeter University.

As it turns out, Cindy has seated me next to her. As we enjoy the tender Christmas ham, we discuss Stonehenge.

Cindy turns and asks me if I'm ready for my surgery.

"I'm not sure you can prepare for surgery for a brain tumor," I reply.

Linda reacts strongly.

"I'm sorry, that's horrible! Have you accepted Jesus Christ as your personal God and Savior?"

I look at Cindy, who gives me a small shrug and a little smile.

I decide to just come out with it.

"Look, Linda, I appreciate your concern, but I'm not a Christian. I go to the Unitarian Church, just like Cindy, and I'm a practicing Buddhist."

Linda looks at me with deep pity.

"If I were having that kind of surgery I would sure want Jesus on my side." She shakes her head slowly.

This is awkward. I have to say something. Impulsively, I tell her about a dream.

"I had a dream about an angel a couple of weeks ago," I offer. "She was beautiful, with her wings folded, with rays of light coming out of her body, kind of a copper color."

Linda reaches over, beaming, and puts her arm around my shoulder.

"You had an angelic visitation! It doesn't matter what you believe, that angel is going to be watching over you!"

THE DAY BEFORE THE DAY
BEFORE

The YMCA is my second home, where I go every day.

I ride half an hour on an exercise bike, watching the scenery that rolls past on the little video screen, looking just like a changing road.

Then I spend another half hour on weight training. I don't lift big amounts, but I do frequent repetitions and have firm, rounded muscles.

Leo, a fellow weight-lifter, a musician with a neat gray mustache, knows how to play more than the violin; he knows the large fifties-era weird-sounding theremin and has told me that you can step through it to change the sound. Hannah, his tall, slender wife, is a concentration camp survivor and has pretty good muscles herself for her advanced age.

Sometimes I talk with the trainers. One is a student working on a master's degree in theology and has a lively sense of curiosity. Another feels that his purpose in life is to persuade me to quit believing in evolution. But both are pleasant and I enjoy passing the time with either.

Next I go upstairs to the indoor track, around noon. Fernando, the rotund janitor, usually picks up his shift about now. He doesn't speak much English. My Spanish is poor, but I know enough to have a limited conversation. He is always interested in news of my father, who suffers from blood cancer. Fernando always smiles when I say Dad has had a good spell.

A sweet little old couple walk together around the track, holding hands. She carries a box of Bible verses in her left hand and frequently mentions Billy Graham. Though I am not a Christian, I agreeably say that I appreciate being blessed, because it's true in a general sense, and it makes them so happy.

I walk for an hour or even more if I have a lot of energy. Then I go downstairs to the cafeteria to get a quinoa salad. "I know, extra avocado!" the woman behind the lunch counter says, knowing that I'm not really supposed to get it.

Today I must tell all these people goodbye.

POP!

In the large lobby of Levine Cancer Institute hospital, I see people standing in line wearing their new Christmas reindeer sweaters and red-and-green striped scarves. Just because I'm nervous, the line is moving slowly. One person is lost, and needs elaborate instructions to an obscure location.

Finally, it's my turn to check in.

"Where are you going?" the person at the desk asks, looking frazzled.

"Pre-op," I say, with a frisson of fear, since this is the day before surgery, and give her my insurance card and credit card to swipe.

The woman points to a room right to one side of the lobby and quickly says "Next?"

I walk slowly over to the pre-op office, as if I could at anytime cancel the whole thing. But of course I have to go in, where a receptionist hands me a clipboard and pen.

"Write down all your medications," she instructs. I pull out the list I keep in my purse. I have a lot of meds, so it takes me some time to tally them. Just as I hand the list to receptionist, someone opens the door and tells me to come in.

31

She takes me into a room, hands me a clipboard, and asks me to write a list of my medications.

"I already did that."

"You have to make a list for the doctor." This makes no sense, but I sense the futility of protesting. I finish the list and sit staring at it for quite a while, maybe twenty minutes, after which a nurse comes in and sits down opposite me.

"What do you take the risperidone for?" she starts.

"Bipolar disorder," I tell her, and she writes something down.

"And what about the gabapentin?"

"MS pain."

She goes through the whole least like this, and mercifully Dr. Wilder comes in when she is nearing the end of the list. She quickly finishes and he sits down at the desk, perusing the paper.

"Okay," he says, "don't eat or drink anything after midnight. Tomorrow you can take the thyroid pill and your risperidone first thing in the morning with a few sips of water, nothing else."

"I get nauseated when I have anesthesia, so will you give me something for that before the surgery?"

"Yes, of course, we can put that in your IV," he offers.

When I leave, I quickly turn back and ask to speak with him. I'm so nervous that I have lost the slip with his instructions. I have to wait until he finishes with another patient.

He enters the waiting room and hands me a new piece of paper with levothyroxine and risperidone scribbled on it.

"And you're going to give me something for nausea, right?" I remind him.

Dr. Wilder sits down next to me on the couch and takes my hand, smiling kindly.

"I've got you," he reassures me. "Stop worrying, I have notes on everything, and I've already sent Dr. Andrews a note telling him what we talked about. You're going to be just fine."

I squeeze his hand, thank him for coming out to see me again, gather my things to go back out to the lobby, and call Don to come from the parking lot to pick me up.

When I slide into the car, he holds his hand out. "Look what I found! I think she's a good luck charm."

It's a small round-headed doll, with fuchsia pigtails and a blue dress showing her name as "Popi." I sit quietly, holding her in one hand all the way home.

When we arrive, I place her on the living room table and look at her for a while. Suddenly I realize that the doll is not named "Popi" at all. Her dress says "Pop" followed by an exclamation mark.

Pop!

Does this mean something?

THE DAY ARRIVES

I follow the instructions. Take a few pills. Pick out some floppy clothing and slip-on shoes. Get in the shower with the special soap liquid.

"Oh, no," I yell. "Look, we don't have nearly enough Hibiclens. There's only enough to cover my chest."

Don has to go to Walgreen's. They don't have it and he has to go to Rite-Aid.

I just sit on the shower stool and drip. It's cold in there. I have no idea why I'm just sitting, waiting passively.

He comes back with a giant pump-bottle of the Pepto-Bismol-color pink gel. I lather it on my whole body, then twice, then start in on a third scrubbing.

"Twice is enough! Please get out and get dressed!" I hear, and at last turn off the comforting flow of hot water.

Clean and dressed, I pack a little bag, like I was going on a short trip. Toothbrush, comb, hand lotion…

"They'll give you hand lotion. Come on, we'll be late. Please be ready when I come to the door."

He always worries about being late. I add a Chapstick. He's outside, warming up the car. He's at the door. There is no more balking. I put on my coat and step out the door, knowing I will come back in some unknown state.

The roads are clear and we get there early. Checking in is easy and we have a long time to wait in a big room packed with other people. How can all these people be getting surgery on the same day?

We see a former colleague, Matt, who comes over to say hello. He and Don talk shop for a few minutes, and then he says his wife is waiting for a third surgery for recurring breast cancer. Her odds are not good.

"What are you here for?" He inquires of me.

"Do you know what a glioma is?"

His face crumbles. "Unfortunately, I do," he says. "Good luck."

"It's getting late. Won't Dr. Andrews be tired? What if he makes a mistake?" I ask Don.

Just then someone opens the door and calls my name. Don and I kiss and I go in.

I'm put in a small room and asked to strip to put on my gown. The lady in there stows my clothes and bag in a locker and leaves.

Dr. Andrews' tall, thin PA comes in, wearing blue surgical scrubs. I suddenly worry about something new and ask if the surgery will aggravate my MS.

"Yes, it certainly could. If you damage any part of the brain you can have inflammation."

He leaves me pondering that, and Dr. Andrews enters.

"Remember you might not be able to talk after this," he reminds me.

Great bedside manner. Gold star and bluebird for Dr. Andrews. Tears spring up but I push them away as someone starts pulling my bed out and down the hall. Damned if I'm going in there crying…

Nothing.

PART TWO

MY NEW WORLD

EMERGING

Why is it so dark? It's like looking through murky river water.

"She's awake," someone says. "Call Beth."

I hear Beth's footsteps but can't make out her face.

"Lift your left foot," she instructs.

That's easy. She goes through a long list of tasks, lifting feet, hand, legs, arms. She's pleased.

"Do you want me to dance the polka too?" I ask. She laughs.

Don rushes up and exclaims "You're talking! You're talking! Your voice is very soft but I can hear you!"

The words are kind of fuzzy but they are definitely speech.

Immense relief and gratitude wash through us.

I'm sleepy and fade out, but someone wakes me, takes me to another room, also murky.

WHOOSHA WHOOSHA WHOOSHA I hear. Oh, okay, I'm getting an MRI.

"Do you want aromatherapy with that?" someone asks. Aromatherapy? This is a dream, but I say yes anyway. Why not?

What just happened? I've been sleeping again. Someone comes and places a cup of soup in front of me. Ugh. I may vomit.

41

I'm so sleepy, why do people keep waking me up? Someone else tries with the soup again and I just turn my head.

"I'm going home to feed and water Salem and clean her litter box," Don announces. Salem! I wonder how Salem, our black cat, is.

"She's fine. She misses you. I won't be long."

It seems like a long time. More sleep. More offers of soup. Don visits twice. How much time has gone by?

"What day is it? What time is it?" I ask. I can't tell whether it's day or night. The lights are still not turned up.

It's 6:00 on Monday.

"How long am I going to be here?" I ask.

A nurse, a new one I don't recognize, hears me and says "We can take you to a regular room if you feel ready. I wish you would eat, but we really can't keep you here forever anyway. I'll call your husband and give him your new room number."

Some time passes. I sleep a little bit then hear "Meredith is being taken out of Intensive Care."

Who says that? Where are they standing?

WHAT KIND OF ANIMAL?

"Great," Don enthuses. "A real room. You're getting better!" He sits on the peculiar, uncomfortable-looking wooden bench provided for visitors, but he isn't complaining.

"Nauseated," I explain. "But good lights here. Weird dream. Aroma."

"Oh, that aromatherapy was real. The MRI person gave it to you—apparently it's a new thing."

Don pauses a moment, and then says, "I think your speech is a bit worse today. This might be that post-op brain swelling they warned us about."

"Why MRI?"

"Because they wanted to make sure the tumor was all out."

Visiting hours end, Don leaves, I refuse another bowl of soup and get ready to call it a night, thinking that I need to go to the bathroom before I fall asleep.

As soon as I stand up, a siren sounds and a strip of red lights come on, whereupon a nurse storms in.

"Get back in bed," she barks. "You have MS and you're a fall risk. You can't get up unless one of us is with you. "

"Gee, thanks," I mutter.

"I'll take you to the bathroom now," she says, "but if you have to go again use the call button."

She watches me pee.

In the ICU, of course they helped me, and Don has gallantly taken me back and forth today, but the idea that I am not allowed to use the bathroom on my own is a rude awakening. I'm about ready to go to sleep but someone knocks on the door and comes in, a young, thin Black woman, carrying a note board.

She introduces herself. "I'm Phyllis. I'm the janitor, but the nurses asked if I would bring this in to you. They like to have the patients draw something they like and write something under it."

Aww. I draw a black animal and write "I love Salem" underneath in blue magic marker.

"What do you call that animal?" I wonder. What kind of creature is Salem? I had no trouble drawing a picture of her but I can't say her species.

Phyllis looks inquisitively as I wring my hands; there is no need for me to say anything at all, but she can tell I want to.

It suddenly pops into my head, and I say triumphantly "Cat!" Salem my cat!"

Phyllis nods and says, "Yes, a beautiful cat."

"You?" I hold out the marker, inviting Phyllis to draw her own picture and she demurs, explaining that it's really for patients.

"Come on," I urge. I want to see what she loves.

She pulls out a photo of two adorable children, a girl and a boy, perhaps five and seven.

"Cute!" I say.

"I have two jobs so they stay with my Mom a lot, but I love on 'em every chance I get."

I like Phyllis but she has to work, and I drift off. Not counting some speech trouble and the bathroom debacle, this has on the whole has been a pretty good day.

POOR PHIL GREEN

The day goes by quietly, as I take a bite of scrambled eggs or a tuna sandwich and look out the window, calm hours with Don catching up on work e-mails. Someone comes around at intervals to give me what seems a large number of pills, but I think at least some of them may be the reason I am not in pain. The strip of bandage winding around my head may itch, but on the whole I am just grateful that I have survived.

Don has been here all day and I can tell he's getting tired, ready to sit in a soft armchair and watch TV, to do something normal.

"You rest," I say to him.

"If you don't mind," he replies, rubbing his forehead, something he does when he's tired. He kisses me, gathers up his laptop, wires, and papers, and leaves for home. Not for the first time, I think that this whole thing has been harder on him than on me.

Evening visiting hours roll around; I'm not expecting anyone and am pleasantly surprised when church friends Joe and Ellie Clark come in my room to visit.

It takes them a couple of minutes to adjust, as Ellie struggles to arrange her ample curves on the unforgiving, orthogonal wood planes.

47

"I've finished the portrait I've been working on," Joe announces, holding out a cell phone snapshot. I smile, seeing a perfect image of a man I met once at a party at Joe's and Ellie's house.

"We're getting a new intern minister," Ellie says, going on to says that she graduated from Harvard's Divinity School.

"Oh, but I do have to tell you about poor Phil Green," Ellie goes on to lament. "You remember when he had a backache? It turned out to be spinal cancer! It's quite aggressive and he may not make it longer than a few weeks. He's on this floor of this hospital, right down the hall and he's asked to see you. Maybe you can find a way to visit."

In our sixties, we no longer use the word "elderly." Phil is probably 75. He plays piano at church, at weddings and funerals, jazz and classical, and he puts wildly imaginative artwork up at our monthly art shows. He has shared his wry short stories with me, about his time as an army psychologist. He makes wry jokes that sneak up on you, take you by surprise, until you say "Oh, my God! That's hilarious!"

There's not much of anything to say after that. They say goodnight soberly, each squeezing my hand as they leave.

More pills. A serving of meat loaf. But sleep will be a while coming, as I lie imaging life without Phil, a life with a big empty spot a mile wide.

DEPARTURES

A nurse comes on the heels of a server carrying a tray with scrambled eggs and toast, which actually look good.

"You can go home today," the nurse tells me. Wonderful. I'm bored and can't wait to get out of here.

"However, we have a rule." Why am I not surprised?

"You have to finish all your food," she admonishes me. "You've just been picking at it."

"Oh, right, Dr. Andrews told you might have few new problems with speech because he's taken you off steroids, which cause some brain swelling. He'll explain it when he comes to see you this evening."

I will certainly have some questions if I can cobble a respectable sentence together.

The day passes by quickly. Don leaves to pack groceries in and catch up on housework. I fill in another flotilla of papers and scarf down a big lunch, chicken, potatoes, a salad, and a container of something which is probably tapioca. Not bad.

Dinner is some dubious fish, bland rice, and under-cooked broccoli. I chew on it and chew on it until I finally finish it. The oatmeal cookies make it worthwhile. Don comes in saying "I

49

have to take a quick nap before Dr. Andrews gets here," and lies down on the bench.

But there is no time for a nap. There is a knock at the door and Dr. Andrews comes in, with his retinue, appearing to be a variety of staff members. Don bolts up and goes over to shake his hand.

"Good evening, Dr. Andrews. Is Meredith going home tonight?"

"Absolutely. We do have to go over a good bit of material first, so you might want to take notes."

Don whips out his trusty phone and Dr. Andrews refers to a clipboard.

"The tumor was malignant, but pathology reports that it's a stage 2 astrocytoma. That's a type of glioma, but this kind is more treatable than some. Your odds are much better."

Don and I break out in cheers.

"But," Dr. Andrews goes on, "I got it out but I had to do a lot of work in Broca's area, where language is produced. I hear that you've been using short sentences and having some difficulty with word finding. I was giving you steroids to reduce swelling, but since your chart says you're bipolar, I've taken you off them and the language problems may get worse for a time."

One of the people traveling with him steps forward. "I'm in charge of speech therapy. I'll see that a speech therapist comes to your house, probably in a couple of weeks."

"Thanks," I say, truly grateful for the help.

I'm getting overwhelmed this but am glad to hear Don is tapping away into his phone to record it.

"Of course you will have radiation and chemotherapy, with treatment starting in a few weeks."

Silence. I know this was coming but still recoil in dread.

Ruth, the Navigator, ends the awkward pause. "Someone will

50

call you about appointments, tell you when the treatments should start, and where you should go. Dr. Arthur is your oncologist and her office will be in touch with you soon."

Can I do all that? There's no alternative.

I say "Thanks" to Dr. Andrews, and Don thanks him profusely for his thorough explanation. An orderly comes in with the wheelchair I will leave in as Dr. Andrews and his team exit.

I'm in the wheelchair, leaving! Going back home, with one last thing to do.

At the nurses' station, I ask Don to explain what that is.

"Look, one of my wife's good friends is here, right on this hall. You know Phil Green? He's asked to see Meredith. He's dying and she wants to say goodbye. Can you please take her to his room?"

Simple enough, you would think.

But no. "You can't do that. There are rules, like, you'd have to get written permission from his family, and his doctor, given the shape he's in," she says. "We just can't do it."

It sinks in that I'm never going to see Phil Green again. I am departing for home to heal, and he is staying to make his final departure.

PART THREE

MY UNFAMILIAR BRAIN

THE WRONG PANTS

My voice may be soft but I can still make my violent reaction to the pants Don has picked out for me to wear on the first day I'm home crystal clear.

They are mud brown, have baggy legs, a stiff wide elastic waist, and pockets that stick out far enough to make me look obese.

"They're ugly."

"Who cares? Nobody is going to see you. They're easy to put on," he cajoles.

"UGLY UGLY UGLY!" I insist.

"Why did you buy them if they're so horrible?" he asks. It's a valid point.

Why did I? I got them in an outlet mall for $7, looking for any elastic waistlines I could during a spell of MS hand impairment. I didn't notice the flaws until I put them on at home the next day. I should have thrown them away immediately.

"Didn't try them on," I mutter.

"But they fit fine! What is your problem? You need to put some clothes on and these fit. PLEASE put them on."

I have no more ammunition. Grumbling, I pull the offending pants on and add a sweater.

"See? Easy. No tight legs, no zippers, no buttons. Thank you!"

Breakfast goes better. Shortly after my diagnosis, we had bought a portable convection oven, which used moving air to distribute heat, to fit on the kitchen island. I had all kinds of ideas about what to cook in it but had trouble figuring out how to use it. Events put the oven low on our list of priorities. But while I was in the hospital Don figured out how to use it to toast English muffins.

He proudly produces four perfect muffins. We sit quietly at the kitchen table, slathering on soft cream cheese.

There is a jar of red stuff in the middle of the table. I would like some of it, but what is it?

"Would you pass the…" I try.

"Jam?" Don says, handing the jar to me. Jam. Of course. I knew that.

MY PILLS ARE MESSED UP

It is bedtime but I can't get to sleep. I turn on the lamp to check on my pills.

I have two pillboxes, one for daytime and another to use at night, plus another small one for things I might need to take at mid-day.

They're mixed up and I can't tell why. Yellow pills, red ones, white ones, and even one fat blue pill, defy order. Maybe I should put the red ones in the morning box.

No, I have to put them back. The red ones are definitely for evening and it's the blue one that belongs in a.m. box, so I shift them, all seven, one at a time.

I take two white ones, but are both at the same time or split between day and night?

Oh, there are so many white ones. I shake the box in frustration.

"What are you doing?" Don protests. "I put your pills in the boxes myself today. They're fine."

"Are they all?"

"Yes. Please turn off your light, you're keeping me awake."

In a few minutes I realize that I put two red ones in the slot for one dose. That can't be right. I turn the light back on and pull the pillboxes out, finding that I also have too many white pills in one box.

"I'm telling you that your pills are okay. Please turn the light out and go to sleep," Don protests.

I close my eyes but sit up again, worried that he must have left something out. Out comes the box again. I start counting furiously—something is surely missing.

"That's it! I'm taking them!" Don roars. He picks all three boxes up, turns off my light, and moves the boxes over to his bedside table.

"But they're messed up," I groan. "Please give them back to me."

"I'll have to rearrange them in the morning as it is. Good night!"

I lie here awake, brooding. I know perfectly well that my pills are messed up.

WHERE IS LUCY?

In winter, bright golden light pours into the living room, suffusing the room with warmth. I sleep a lot on the couch, dozing and waking, dozing and waking, Salem curled up in the curve of my belly.

Lucy, Don's daughter, sits quietly on the opposite couch, not trying to talk to me, just smiling gently.

She is beautiful, with bright blue eyes and flowing brown air. Lucy rarely dresses up when visiting, though, wearing jeans and tee shirts with one or another colorful emblem. She is as sharply intelligent as her father and we have had some wonderful conversations, but it's enough now for her to sit with me, smiling gently.

A few days go by like this as I drift into and out of seep.

Today as I head back to the couch from our usual morning cream-cheese muffins, I don't see Lucy.

"Don, where is Lucy?

"Meredith, you know that Lucy lives in Japan. Why are you asking?" Don wonders.

"No, earlier, here…"

"She's in Japan now! She hasn't been here at all!"

I look at the empty couch. I miss her.

TRANSPORT

I'm standing on my desk, spreading my wings out and preparing for liftoff. I flap my wings, decide to cross the room, and leap.

"OOOWWWW!"

Don is standing next to me, asking what happened.

"Flying," I cry. "Hit the wall."

"No, you're not flying," he sighs. "You're on the bathroom floor. You fell. What hurts?"

"I CAN fly," I wail. "Just crashed."

He sighs again. "Tell me where it hurts."

"Side."

"Left or right?"

"Left."

He feels. "Ah, ribs. Couple of ribs. They'll hurt for a while." Pulling me up, he moves me back to bed and we sleep for a few more hours.

Around nine he gently helps me into the car, me whimpering and holding my side. He patiently shepherds me into the Urgent Care for X-rays.

"Two broken ribs," pronounces the emergency doctor. "They'll heal in a few weeks."

ONCOLOGY

This is January 11th, my first visit to Dr. Arthur, my oncologist. She is a cancer specialist and will be in charge of my treatment from now on.

We drive to Levine Cancer Institute again, finding the usual throngs of sick people—people who are bald and skinny, people in wheelchairs or on crutches, along with the healthy-looking people who are helping them get around. But I am pleased to see many patients, carrying papers and orders, in the crowd look normal, proof that cancer does not necessarily cause radically altered appearance.

The first order of business is to sign in, which takes a surprisingly short time. Then we go to the lab, where someone amazingly quickly takes blood using my port, sparing me a barrage of needle sticks. It seems that IV ports are common for cancer patients who receive IV chemotherapy.

Then we take the elevator upstairs to the 5th floor and wait for an hour. Reading being laborious, I am bored, inspect the room, and observe that there is a barf bag dispenser on the wall, really high-tech ones like balloons rather than the flimsy paper ones on airplanes. Fortunately, no one is using one right now.

I look at my watch. The receptionist says "I'm sorry for the wait. Dr. Arthur must have someone who's having a hard time. She's often late but that's because she takes however long she needs."

There is a *Scientific American* on the table, and I decide to at least try reading. I look at an article about evolution, a topic I've studied extensively.

I concentrate hard, but the words are indecipherable, and I have to re-read the article. I have to admit that, while I can confirm that the scientific method had been used in the study, I have no idea what it's really about or what kind of conclusion had been arrived at.

This confirms my suspicion but is still a bitter disappointment. Not only is *Scientific American* my favorite magazine, but I am proud of my Bachelor of Science degree from the College of William and Mary. I brood until someone opens the door and calls my name.

We stand up and go in, me wheeling myself in on my wheel-barrow like Rollator. Like Dr. Andrews, Dr. Arthur travels with a gaggle of other health-care professionals. I don't even try to keep up with this crew.

Dr. Arthur is stunning. She has enviable cheekbones and long golden hair and is wearing a flowered designer dress. I was expecting someone more gloomy. She's smiling, showing perfect teeth. I'm over-awed.

She's friendly too!

"Your MRI is good. Is your scar healing all right?" she begins.

In answer, I flip the hair above the horse-kick mark on the left side of my head.

"Good!" she exclaimed. "That means we can get started with radiation and chemotherapy!"

"What...already?"

She scribbles something on my chart and explains that radiation will start on the 22nd, after I have a mask fitted to keep the radiation focused on the exact area of the scar.

"Also, I want you to take a small oral dose of Temodar, which is chemotherapy, two hours before the radiation," she instructs. "It should not cause you any problems."

So we're jumping in with both feet for sure. The idea of radiation fills me with fear, but her words also fill me with hope. I will be able to do something to actually fight the cancer. Am I ready?

ALIEN

January 14, the day I'm going to have my radiation mask made, has come. Sandra, who is head of our Unitarian church's Care Committee, is here to take me.

This is a big project. I have to go out to the porch, where Don sits me on the front stairs, carries the Rollator to ground level, maneuvers me down the stairs and back in the rollator so I can walk myself down to the driveway and crawl into Sandra's SUV, and finally stows my chariot into the back. In these last few weeks, I've been coming to understand that this whole thing may be harder on him than me.

"Thanks, I know that was hard," I say, squeezing his hand.

"Glad to do it," he responds, panting a little.

Sandra is surprisingly strong for her size. She wrestles the rollator out so I can push myself into the sunlit waiting room and introduce myself to the receptionist.

"Ms. Merritt is here for her fitting," she says, and just as Sandra and I sit down, a technician comes to take me back. Sandra settles down with an issue of *Bon Appetit*.

"Today you won't have a treatment, we're just going to make a helmet to keep your head still when we use the radiation beam," she explains. "You'll lie on the gantry and we'll fit thermoplastic material over your head, back and neck."

"What is a gantry?"

"Oh, that's what we call the table you lie on. I'm sorry it's cold and hard, it's just that we need to have your head completely flat."

I put on the gown she gives me. She's right, it's pretty Spartan. The technician comes in with another person, who shows me a big square of plastic mesh.

"This is thermoplastic," she explains. "I'm going to soak it in hot water and mold it around your head, and then you just have to lie still for about 15 minutes for it to mold itself to you."

The plastic is hot, though not too hot, but it's hard to lie there not moving or talking. Finally the timer goes over and I start to sit up.

"Oh no, stay still! We have to do a simulation treatment and mark your mask to show where to aim the beam."

The technicians mold my mask and add bolts to the bottom it. This is beginning to feel creepy.

The X-ray machine buzzes and laser lights flash, but this is just more lying still and waiting. At the end of this, I can sit up for her to pull the mask off. She hands it to me so I can have a look.

I see my face, which appears small and delicate, on the front, and then an expansive sweep of plastic, extending way back about a foot.

It looks like fantastic creature. It looks like an alien's head. A beautiful alien.

HAZARDOUS MATERIALS

Tomorrow is the first radiation treatment. This afternoon, a delivery truck pulls up in front of our front yard and lets its driver out, who trots up to the door.

He hands me a small box and asks me to sign for it.

"It's your Temodar, from Levine's Specialty Pharmacy," he explains. "This is what Dr. Arthur called in."

We open the box and find a bottle of pills labeled "TOXIC" in large letters, along with an instruction leaflet and a regular bottle of non-toxic nausea pills.

"Do not touch Temodar," the pamphlet begins. "Wear gloves at all times when handling Temodar. Discard gloves safely, and wash your hands when you have completed administration. Do not chew Temodar."

I'm surprised that the bottle isn't marked with a skull and cross-bones.

Don goes to Walgreen's, returning with a box of latex gloves and a container of little plastic cups. He commandeers a small antique cabinet from the front hall and sets it up in the bathroom, right next to the sink, where he can wash.

I have serious concerns about the fact that it isn't safe for Don to touch it but it is fine for me to swallow it.

DYSARTHRIA

So far, despite my stumbling over and searching for words, I've found that I can usually make my thoughts and wishes clear. Today, when Don asks how I am, he has to ask me twice.

"Wad wadn't speekin verwell."

"You sound drunk. What's wrong?" Don asks.

"Donnow wors messup."

"Well," he says, "we have to leave now for your appointment to see Dr. Simmons anyway; if he doesn't know what this is he can tell us who might help."

He calls ahead and asks the nurse to tell him I'm slurring my speech.

Dr. Simmons, my psychiatrist, comes into the lobby to get us and shows us into his office, where a transparent model of a brain, with parts showing inside, sits on the desk. Dr. Simmons is a compassionate man, always wearing a sympathetic smile, and he looks kindly at me today.

"Hi, Meredith. Can you tell me what's going on?"

"Slurrin...wors jumblinup," I explain.

He pulls out my chart and looks at the new lab report.

"Your lithium level was 1.0 when you had this blood test the other day," he notes. "That's not quite toxic, but it's as high as it can go without being toxic, and it may have gone up. You have so many things going on, MS, bipolar disorder, and brain surgery. Any of them could cause speech problems, but I think you must have some brain swelling and oversensitivity to drugs. Surgery can cause dehydration, lithium can cause dehydration, and that alone could contribute to your problem. Let's try cutting the lithium down to half. I think you came to the right place."

I digest his comments about lowering the lithium, and I feel worried about the reduction..

"Whaff I ... gget realler ... real..."

I fish for what I want to say. Finally, I say "sad."

He takes his glasses off, rubs his eyes, puts them back on.

"You could get depressed," he admits.

Depressed. That's the word I was looking for.

"We'll keep checking it frequently, though. I doubt you'll crash," he goes on.

I feel exposed. Either depression or mania would be a disaster in the middle of everything that's going on now and the higher dose of lithium had been keeping both at bay.

I look at Dr. Simmons and he looks at me.

"It's the only safe thing to do. The level is really high," he says. "I'll be here if you need me."

PART FOUR

FIRE

BOMB

My head is bolted to the gantry, the newly-crafted helmet gripping my face tightly. I am looking straight overhead to a scene of forest trees. It's very soothing.

The technician hums quietly as she moves around.

"Don't move. Just relax," she instructs. "This will take about fifteen minutes."

She places a machine up to the left side of my head, pointing it at my scar, and presses a button. A bright beam of light comes on. The device doesn't make a lot of noise, just kind of a hiss.

I'm not fooled. I know that suns are blazing, that the fiery winds of crashing particles are hurtling into the site of my tumor, ripping electrons off right and left. All the fury of a bomb that can blow a city off the earth is smashing into any cancer cells that dare to linger.

A TOUR OF EGYPT

My speech therapist, Anya, sent from the home care department of the hospital, sits across from me on the couch, balancing a fat notebook on her lap.

"I'm Anya, your speech therapist for seven sessions, meeting once a week, starting today, but I can't guarantee it's going to be the same time of day. Will that work out for you?"

"That's fine. Just understand sometimes I speak better than others."

"I have exercises for you to do. I'm not grading you, so don't worry if you have difficulty," she starts.

I'm eager to have a chance to start working on my problem. I'm used to talking freely with other people and the struggle to find the right word is getting old.

"I understand you have difficulty finding the correct word to use. So let's begin with identifying some animals," she goes on. "I'll describe an animal and you tell me what it is. The first question is: This large animal is white and lives in the Arctic."

Well, of course it's a polar bear. We go on to rabbits, which hop and have long ears, and whales, which are the longest animals in the sea.

But then she says "This animal has a very long neck."

I think about this for a while. Camels have long necks, but then so do llamas.

"How about llamas?"

"Hmm," Anya muses. "They do have long necks, but I was thinking about a giraffe." A giraffe? Of course. How could I have forgotten "Giraffe?"

But we continue until we reach the last of the list of animals, and I only make one other error.

"Okay, you're doing pretty well with finding animal words. Let's move on to something different."

She reads a story: "Of the seven wonders of the world, the one that has not been destroyed is the pyramids in Egypt. They were built as tombs for the kings nearly 5,000 years ago. The pyramid built for Cheops is located near Cairo. It is 450 feet high and 758 feet in length across the bottom, which is equivalent to about three city blocks."

I'm surprised. I thought speech therapy would be all about words.

She hands me a clipboard with the story and the list of questions. I read the story again. It sounds like a fourth-grade geography lesson.

The first question is:

> The story is about:
> Egyptians
> Tombs
> Wonders of the World
> Pyramids

How can I pick just one? The paragraph has Egyptians, tombs, Wonders of the World, and Pyramids all over the place.

I look at Anya, puzzled, and shake my head.

Her smile is friendly. "It's Pyramids. Never mind, we'll start with something easier next week."

I'm still thinking about the Pyramids as she leaves. I'm pretty sure there is no one correct answer. But there must be. I think about it for fifteen minutes and haven't got a clue. I have a hard time remembering the numbers, too. I finish my first speech therapy with only puzzlement.

POISON

One night, after only several sessions of radiation I can't stop throwing up. This reminds me of the "24 hour bug" small children fall prey to, consigning hapless parents to a night of holding the head of a puking child.

Don is holding onto my shoulders as I empty my stomach again.

"So I'm so sore sorry," I croak.

"Don't try to talk. You're really sick and we're going to see Dr. Arthur first thing in the morning. Do you think you could try to sleep?"

I am tired, but every time I drift off, nausea grips me again and I head back to the bathroom. It feels like I'm bringing up poison.

Maybe this is caused by Temodar. It must be.

By morning I am not vomiting but am having trouble holding my head up. My hands shake violently.

I'm not asleep but somehow not awake either. I feel Don lifting me down the stairs, turning me so I'm sitting on the rollator for him to push me using its handlebars.

Although I'm fading in and out, I realize that we have at last arrived at Dr. Arthur's office.

"She made room for you," the receptionist says.

Dr. Arthur doesn't even wait for us to come in. She steps out, takes one look, and cries "Emergency Room. Now!"

Someone comes with a chair. I drift into a fog as they begin to wheel me away.

WONDROUS LOVE

It's dark. I'm alone. Wait. There are other people over there. What are they doing? There's a doctor.

The doctor looks confused, trying to figure something out, talking with the group of immigrants with him. They carry blankets with Middle Eastern designs and talk all at once in a language I don't know. The baffled physician crowds them into one cubicle and leaves.

This is a hospital emergency room of course. Something has happened to me; I have brain cancer and I'm in a hospital.

There is no privacy, so that I can clearly see into the cubicle the doctor puts the people into, where the light stays on. They're talking, gesticulating, and walking around, while drinking from what look like jugs of tea.

A nurse stops by my bed and asks how I'm feeling now. I can't make coherent speech, and I grit my teeth because I can understand her perfectly.

Now the other people are going to sleep in a ball of human forms, arm over shoulder, foot over leg, intertwined, making a sphere of affection. Am I dreaming? No, even though I have never seen this form of sleeping, I am fully awake and aware. How much they love each other!

More nurses come and go, turning the lights on, asking me more questions—How am I feeling? What's going on? When is my husband coming back?

I try again to answer them, but my words tumble out of my mouth without meaning. The nurses frown, purse their lips, shake their heads. "I don't understand what you're trying to say," they reply. Collecting tubes of blood, they tell me nothing.

Morning comes and Don returns, having been able to get a well-deserved full night of sleep. When he appears, the doctor comes over to talk to us.

"You're having a toxic reaction to at least one of your medications because of interaction with your chemotherapy," he explains. "So we'll keep you for a couple of days to figure out what we need to drop."

The doctor moves across the room and begins examining the old woman with the immigrants' group whom I suppose to be the grandmother, having finally guessed what's going on. He says something I can't hear, but one of the nurses responds by giving her an injection and handing her a bottle of pills, and the family files out, rejoicing.

While I'm being transported to my room, I remain enthralled by the scene I've just witnessed, the compassion this immigrant family has shown among themselves, while struggling to be understood and searching for the cause of an unknown illness. As the old hymn says, "What Wondrous Love Is this, Oh My Soul?"

THIS IS NOT MY ROOM

After my long night in the ER, I'm exhausted and slip into a blissful sleep.

It seems that only a moment has passed when I wake up and find a nurse standing next to me, pushing a pole with a blood pressure cuff and a device for measuring temperature.

I look at the clock and see that, in fact, only a moment has passed since I went to sleep.

"I just need to check your vitals," the nurse explains.

I've become accustomed to the fact that when you are in the hospital you can expect to be disturbed every couple of hours with this ritual, day or night. It's so important to them.

It seems that I'm still alive, but I'm also wide awake. That's okay, here come the blood people, with charts of medication I take.

"Let's see what happens when we give her this," one of them says to the other, handing me a cup holding a pill. I swallow it as they draw a vial of blood from my IV port.

"Okay, let's check the level in four hours," they agree, just as Don is coming in with a Starbucks cup and a bagel.

"I've heard that Dr. Simmons and Dr. Johnson talked with

each other this morning. The hospital called both of them and they think some of your medications have interacted with the Temodar. Your lithium is too high again and there is a problem with something else," he sighs. "Your brain has become super-sensitive to drugs."

A nurse comes in to introduce herself. "I'm Salamandarina, I'll be on the morning shift."

"Hi, Sa sal…"

I stop short, aware that I was about to say "Salamander." My speech is still hard to call up.

"Don't worry," she laughs. "We're working on resolving your blood toxicities."

"The doctor will be coming in to talk to you all," Salamadarina says. Why, I wonder, does she not go by Sally?

The doctor looks like he hasn't slept in a week. Maybe he hasn't.

"Dr. Simmons says that you can't take any lithium at all, in any dosage, and Dr. Johnson says your Gabapentin is toxic as well. You have to drop both completely."

No lithium at all? Will I have a major depression? And Gabapentin? It reduces nerve pain in MS. Why are these things that have helped so much suddenly toxic? This seems unfair.

The doctor, rumpled as he is, looks professional when he says "You'll adjust. It will take the rest of today for your blood to clear the drugs, and we'll do an MRI just to be safe. Your speech will regularize once we've titrated your blood. You can go home tomorrow morning."

Another night? I would really like to go now and see Dr. Simmons and Dr. Johnson myself.

Don is a little restless. "I'm going to run to campus for a while, do some shopping and laundry, and take care of Salem. Do you mind if I just stay home tonight and come back to pick you up in the morning? We can just make your radiation appointment."

I nod, and he gives me a kiss good-bye.

It's late afternoon before someone shows up to take me to the MRI machine, an athletic woman who puts me in a wheelchair and pushes me vigorously down a dizzying number of corridors, wheels me into and out of several elevators. I could not find my way back with a trail of breadcrumbs.

When the MRI is finished, she re-appears and takes me through the labyrinth again.

When she wheels me into a room, I'm not sure where I am. I don't recognize anything.

I see Salamadrina and ask her where I am. My voice is semi-functional now.

"You're back in your room," she says, puzzled.

"No, not. Not my roo room!" I insist.

She shows me my bag, points to the chalkboard where they have written my name.

I feel dislocated, adrift in a wide ocean. Nothing looks right. I just watch for a while, trying to put the pieces together.

That is my bag. I do remember the chalkboard. My name is on it.

I guess it is my room after all.

THE SEAMSTRESS

This morning I can go home from the hospital. Being in the hospital has become a part of my life, but it is such a trial, making me feel like a zoo animal. I hear Don coming down the hall and quickly shed my gown to pull on the jeans and T-shirt I came in, shove my personal items in the bag that goes everywhere with me, and slide on my clogs.

"Bye, thanks!" I wave at Salamandarina, still not saying her name. She gives me the usual discharge papers and brings my rollator. If we are quick, we can reach the radiation center in time to meet today's appointment, so we sign out at the desk right away and head straight for the car.

Perfect. Radiation goes smoothly, as it always does, and I'm looking forward to getting home and snuggling with Salem. I miss her so much when I'm not at home.

But...what's this? I've just taken my gown off and see that there is no band-aid on my IV port and there are weird little strings hanging down from it.

An IV port is a device implanted in the chest above the heart, called a central line, which allows blood to be drawn out or liquid medication to be injected directly into the bloodstream. Many

89

people who receive frequent blood tests or intravenous infusions and have poor veins in their hands or arms use these devices. The procedure involves "accessing" and "de-accessing," using needles to get in and withdrawing needles to get out. A port has to remain flushed with heparin (to prevent clotting) and closed between uses as it is easily infected if not cared for properly.

I call Sarah, the radiation technician and ask her to look at my port.

"What in the world? What are all those little strings? It looks like it was sewn in!" she exclaims. "Hey, Dina, come over here!"

Dina, the nurse, takes one look and says "Whoever did this failed to de-access it and it's wide open. And I've never seen anything like these strings. We have to get you to the Infusion Center right away before it gets infected."

The Infusion Center is where I go regularly for MS medication, so this should be straightforward. I think.

Dina has Carol, the head nurse, on the phone.

"Yes," I hear Carol saying, "but we have rules about doing things that aren't part of our procedures. We know her and this is embarrassing, but we're not supposed to do anything like that."

Dina snaps. "Look, my patient is frail and elderly, you have to take care of this."

Poor Carol. Poor Dina. Poor me. I'm starting to worry.

"Um, yeah, let me ask the manager for an exception…"

I hear Carol's voice on the phone again. "Okay, but we're closing in an hour so she has to get there before then."

Don drives like a master cabbie, but it's not a sure thing. We arrive at the Infusion Center 10 minutes before closing time.

Carol apologizes for the confusion and quickly starts to work on the port.

"What are these strings? It looks like suture thread!"

She pulls the strings out, disinfects everything, runs heparin through the port, applies a band-aid to the site, and sighs deeply.

"Thank you so much, I don't what might have happened otherwise," I breathe.

I resist the temptation to ask Carol if she thinks I am really "elderly and frail." I can't be. What a notion.

WHERE IS THAT WORD?

"I hear you've hit some trouble," Anya remarks, looking worried. "Tell me about it."

"Yeah, I had a toxic reaction to chemo and ended up in the hospital, but I'm okay now," I explain. "Speaking a bit better."

"Great! Are you ready to work?"

"Yes, the hospital is a pretty boring place."

She smiles. "Right now, let's go! What do you think is your biggest problem at this point?"

"Word finding," I say without a doubt. "It takes me forever to pull up the word I want to say. It's like there's a blank in the space where I want to say something. But it's inconsistent."

Anya pulls out a few exercise sheets and says "I'm going to show you some pictures and you tell me what they are."

The first one seems easy because it has bristles. Not a toothbrush, though. It's larger.

"Hairbrush?"

"Yes. What is this?"

I've just finished putting my dishes away, and this is what I used: "A sink."

The next one was even easier. "Who could miss a clock?"

But now I have in front of me a wedge-shaped object with a big handle. As I inspect it, I can see that it's made of metal; the material looks shiny. Gold, silver, aluminum, iron...Iron! "It's an iron, Anya!"

"This one took you quite a while, but you eventually got it. Can you tell me the steps you took?" she asked.

When I explained, she nodded and said, "Yes, okay, you did this one using associations. That's a good strategy when you're stuck. But maybe we should move on to a different task."

Shuffling her papers, she calls out "This large animal is white and lives in the Arctic."

"Polar bear," I answer immediately.

This animal has long ears, hops, and lives in the forest."

"Rabbit."

"This flying rodent lives in caves and attics."

"Bat."

"You're not having any trouble at all with this exercise!" Anya exclaims. "I see what you mean by inconsistent."

"It's because I'm an animal person. I was doing animal science even before grade school and I was a volunteer at the zoo."

"Hmm, your interest in animals makes it easy for you to identify them. I wonder if this is because you're wired for it. Interesting. Of course, it's also possible that you're just good at this type of question. The brain is full of mysteries."

Between my double major in biology and psychology and my direct experience of brain pathology, I agree wholeheartedly. "We'll never know," I say.

Despite the circumstances, I have to admit it's a miracle that human communication goes on in the first place.

CATS ON THE RUN

This is Anya's third visit.

"Let's do some memory exercises," she suggests. "The first time we tried it, you had trouble, we need for you to challenge yourself."

"Okay." Back to stories. It seems that speech therapy really is more about riddles than talking.

"Here is another story. I'll read it to you and you need to answer some question about it."

"Lindsey is in her second year of college," Anya states. "She has to take history, literature, and biology classes. She is an excellent student."

Anya stops there and asks "What classes is Lindsey taking?"

This one, unlike the one with the Egyptians, is easy.

"History, literature, and biology."

"Great! Let's do one that's a little harder." She has pulled out a new page from her notebook and reads:

"After dinner he had to clean up. He washed and dried the dishes. He put the silverware in the drawer and the plates in the cabinet. Then he dried out the sink and hung up the towel."

"Okay," I agree.

"So, what did he put in the drawer?" she queries.

"Silverware."

"What did he put in the cabinet?"

"Plates." This is going pretty well.

"Fine. This one is a little longer."

She reads:

"Kris' Samoyed dog, Fluffy, needs a lot of care. Fluffy has long white hair so she needs to be combed every day. In order to see that she gets enough exercise, Kris takes Fluffy for a long walk in the park. Fluffy likes to stand in creeks and lakes. It makes her feel cooler. Fluffy is a great companion."

"Why must Fluffy be combed every day?"

Hmm. I'm getting tired. But I answer anyway.

"She has long white fur."

"Did it say fur?"

"Umm, hair."

"Right," Anya goes on. "Where do they go for walks?"

I pause. "By ponds and lakes."

"Well, they do, but where do they go first?" Anya prompts.

"Oh, right, to the park."

"One more, What does Fluffy like to do?"

"Oh, I know. Chase cats!"

"I think you're getting tired. Fluffy likes to do what else?"

Oh, right. "She stands in the water to get cool."

"Good, you got it!"

But really, I have never known a dog who just stood around in the water. Fluffy is weird.

PUZZLES

Anya comes in with a new notebook and says she wants to work on syntax today, which sound a bit daunting.

"What exactly is syntax?" I inquire.

"Syntax is the order words come in, like saying 'Barking is the dog' instead of the correct version 'The dog is barking,'" she says, laying out a pile of cardboard squares with words written on them. "Try to put this pile together."

Scattered in front of me I see "George," "cool," "window," "the," "to," "opens," and "be."

I line the words up to read "George opens the door cool to be." Does this sound okay? I think so.

Anya tells me to switch "cool" and "to be." I see immediately what I have done.

"Now try another."

She puts the words "refrigerator," "milk," "of," "put" and "carton," "in," and "the" down.

"Put. The milk. Carton. In. Refrigerator," I mumble, before lining the words up as "Put the carton of milk in the refrigerator."

"Good. Now let's try one as fast as you can."

She puts down "book," "is" "pictures," "with," "easy," "to", "quickly," "read."

I find it easy to move the words to lay out "The book with pictures is easy to read quickly."

"Exactly," Anya says with a big smile.

"We do three more, only one on which I linger. Words are beginning to flow together.

"Okay, that's enough for today. Whenever you falter, remember the secret to syntax is if doesn't sound right, it probably isn't."

As she leaves and I begin for my radiation session, I feel a warm sense of fulfillment. This has been a good day.

SISTERS

The way radiation has been working is that one of the women from church come to our house, Don pulls my rollator down the stairs and into their cars, reversing the process when I come back. So far, though, everyone has been able to move the device when we get to the radiation building. I think Martha, who is the chair of the Care Committee, has been arranging rides with strong women who have station wagons or SUV's.

Radiation has been going on for nearly six weeks. The ladies who have been taking me always sit with me while I'm waiting. I have enjoyed their company very much; the routine is the same every day, and would be tedious if they had not been there.

Sandy is taking me today. Since working with Anya, I have been able to make simple sentences and find more words, and I enjoy being able to have a conversation.

"How are feeling about your cancer?" I ask Sandy. She has certainly discussed it with me before, but it was so traumatic that we often return to the topic.

"I really miss my job," she says. She had been working as a vitamin and supplement advisor in the store Earthfare, which carries natural foods and other natural products, such as cruelty-free cos-

99

metics and makeup. She was let go when she had been diagnosed. She was very good at the job.

"It's a shame they didn't just give you a leave of absence and hire a temp," I say.

"I still think that was unfair."

Just then Beth, one of the assistants, comes out to the waiting room.

"Meredith, we're ready for you," she calls, and I get my rollator out. Sandy picks up her book. She has good taste in literature and is half-way through "The Heart Is a Lonely Hunter" by Carson McCullers.

The radiation room is spare, pretty much just the gantry and a row of helmets like mine. Although they don't specialize in brain radiation, it seems that brain cancer is relatively common.

Beth bolts my helmet on and positions my head, all the way talking about her weekend commutes to Virginia to be with her husband. She likes her work and the people she works with so that she doesn't mind the extra travel.

She and Andrea and the technician fit my helmet on, slide me in, and switch the radiation on. I'm thinking about Sandy and worry if the beam could cause me to develop breast cancer, even though I've been told that it could not.

Beth returns me to Sandy and we go back to the house.

"Want to come in?" I ask as Don retrieves my rollator.

"Sure," Sandy says, following us into the living room.

But my speech begins disintegrating and soon I can't hold my end of the conversation up, beginning to doze.

"Cccan't ... say," is all I can manage.

"Okay, I'd better let you rest," Sandy says.

I am almost asleep before Sandy closes the front door.

NUMBER HASH

Anya and I have fallen into the pattern of word identification and questions about stories. Today we are doing clues to what a word might be.

"What word goes with 'batteries, bright, and bulb'?"

"Light? Wait a minute…" I say and pause.

"You're pretty close," Anya encourages me.

"Oh. A flashlight."

"Good, you did a good job saying what specific kind of light it is. What tipped your mind?"

"Batteries."

"That's good," Anya says. "You waited to think about all the details."

Fingers, palm, and wrist equals "hand." Write, lead, and eraser equal "pencil."

"You're good with these. Let's move onto stories," she says.

"Bob and Terri's original home loan was for 30 years at 10% interest," Anya begins. "Five years into the loan, they refinanced at 8 1/2% interest for 30 years. Two years later they were able to refinance for 15 years at 6 ½% interest."

10%? These stories were written a long time ago!

"Are you ready for some questions?" Anya suggests.

"Fire away."

"What kind of loan did Bob and Terri originally have?"

Long pause. "Twenty, sorry thirty years."

"How much interest did they originally pay on their house?"

I think for a minute. "Thirty?"

"No, that was how many years the loan was for. Want to try again?"

I fish in my mind. "Ten percent?" I'm not sure.

"Yes. The next question is 'When they refinanced the first time how much was their interest?'"

Eight something? Maybe so.

When I submit 8 as my answer, Anya frowns.

"These questions shouldn't be so hard," she observed. "Last time you did one exercise which was supposed to be on that level without any difficulty."

"Numbers. Hate numbers," I offer as my excuse.

I can't figure out how to write down a phone number without making mistakes until the other person says they will text it. I can't remember how much I've spent when I order two things on Amazon.

"I think you have dyscalcula. That's like the hard time you have with words, but with numbers. It's a parietal function! Your tumor was temporal."

She's very curious and asks if she can text the nurse at Dr. Arthur's office. I'm curious too. Anya's next appointment has been canceled and she doesn't mind waiting. Dr. Arthur's staff is very efficient about following their texts; after half an hour Libby texts back "Your tumor bordered on the parietal lobe."

Well. More damage than I originally thought. Maybe somebody forgot to tell me, but it's also likely that they did and I forgot.

But do I need numbers anyway?

CONTESTED NOODLES

Ellie wants to take me to lunch. We haven't seen each other lately, since she broke her leg. Now she can move around, but since her husband takes their car to work she gets around by Uber.

The car arrives and I see that someone else is in there. She didn't mention bringing anyone else.

Ellie rolls down the window, waves with a meaty arm, and yells "I brought Lila!"

Lila! She quit calling me last fall when I misunderstood the date of something she wanted to do. In fact, she hung up on me. Later she sent an e-mail saying that she didn't have time for someone so scattered.

I'm tired today, which makes my speech worse, so it's a strain even to ask how either of them are. I just say "Ladies." Ellie talks enough to cover a lot of silence. She's carrying on about her alcoholic brother in LA, who apparently is in a lot of trouble.

We arrive at P. F. Chang's and busy ourselves getting inside the door, Ellie and I both using canes, taking our seats, ordering food, and going to the ladies' room, but the time arrives when we have to look at each other, Ellie at the head of the table and Lila across from me.

"I hear you have cancer," Lila says. "You look really weak."

"Physical …" I reply.

"Physical what?" she queries. I fish in my mind.

"Physical therapy," I finally reply.

To Ellie, she says "Aren't you going to take off your hat?"

"I always wear my hat!" Ellie protests. It has sequins all around the brim — quirky, but quirks are just Ellie. She may look a little weird, but that's part of her charm.

The food arrives. Lila has ordered only a bowl of wonton soup and I have Hunan shrimp. Now, Ellie is a big girl, Ellie is a hungry girl, and she has a heaping plate of orange chicken and a large side order of noodles.

Lila reaches out for the noodles and slides the plate down the table, out of Ellie's reach.

Ellie looks at Lila, stunned.

I reach over and move the noodles back to Ellie.

Staring at Lila, I smile. I don't say a word. My voice is better, but everybody knows I'm in the middle of speech therapy so I have an excuse for not speaking.

CABBAGE HEAD

Anya is showing me pictures of food today.

"What do you think this is?" she asks.

That's easy. It's a hot dog – long, red, in a bun, smeared with yellow mustard.

"Hot dog," I answer.

"Great! How about this one?"

Corn, of course, rows of little yellow kernels.

"Corn."

I'm on a roll.

Then I see the next one. It's green. Okay, but what is it? It's shaped like a head. It has leaves. It looks kind of like lettuce. But I'm not sure.

"Lettuce?" I venture.

Anya says "No, this one is cabbage."

Cabbage!

I like cabbage. Maybe Don could pick some at the store for supper.

PROGRESS

The hospital specified that my insurance would cover seven speech therapy sessions and this is my last. I hope I will do well on this lesson.

"I'm going to challenge you a little with a few more complex stories, and then I'm going to evaluate you." Anya started. "Let's try this one."

"Each day, Paul drank one cup of coffee before, during, and after breakfast. Before long, he began to feel nervous and jittery, and he had trouble sleeping at night. When he switched to decaffeinated coffee, his problems went away."

"Let's do the first question: What does Paul drink every day?"

"Coffee," I answer.

"How many cups does he drink every day?"

I pause, but only briefly. The number comes up! "Three."

"Right! How about how Paul began to feel when he drank coffee?"

"Nervous and jittery," I answer.

On good days, my mind works better; this is clearly an improvement. This is probably due to the fact that we have started earlier than we usually do.

"What did he have trouble doing at night?" she asks.

"Did he have to switch to decaffeinated coffee?"

"Yes," I answer confidently.

"Did Paul drink four cups of coffee a day?"

Hmm. Maybe. "Yes. No. Three."

"Good save", Anya says. Now try "Does Paul sleep well now?"

"Yes!" I crowed, "I did it!"

Anya takes out a sheet of paper and goes through examples of the kind of exercise she has been giving me, and she is pleased.

"You've really improved. You should be proud. Now you don't need me any more, except for one piece of advice. You can use telegraphic speech when you get stuck. That means you use the simplest elements of what you want to say. Telegraphic speech often occurs as a symptom, but you can do it yourself to take a shortcut when you are stuck."

She gives me a warm hug goodbye, and packs up her things, both of us smiling.

THE CLOUD OF UNKNOWING

Radiation is finished and we head to Dr. Arthur's office to find out what comes next. I know it's chemotherapy, but I'm not sure in what form and am feeling pretty nervous.

Dr. Arthur looks very serious and says "Now we have to make some big changes."

"Now you're going to triple your dose of Temodar, taking it for seven days consecutively every month, for six months."

That sounds like a lot of Temodar. One pill a day had only made me feel only occasionally queasy, rarely actually sick, so that I haven't used very many of the nausea pills, Zofran, but now I'm worried.

"We're going to give you more Zofran, too," she adds. "You'll probably need two twice a day."

We get up and head for the door, pondering this transition from one stage of treatment to the next.

"What is my prognosis?" I ask.

Dr. Arthur's smile fades.

"I don't know," she answers. "It can recur and we don't know a lot about astrocytoma in the first place. I wish I had something better to tell you but I honestly don't."

She rises spontaneously and gives me a hug, her brow furrowed.

I think of the medieval text "The Cloud of Unknowing," in which the anonymous author seeks to attain union with the Divine without a shred of evidence the Divine even exists at all.

This is a kind of hope that may seem to be naïve, but in a split second I decide to nurture that kind of faith in the likelihood of my own survival and recovery.

THE SHOALS

This is the seventh day of Temodar, two giant capsules, which arrived with the usual warnings for Don to assemble them with gloves and for me the same injunction to swallow them without letting them sit in my mouth. In large letters, the bottle instructs that the pills are not to be chewed.

I wonder what would happen if I did chew Temodar? I don't wonder enough to put it to the test.

The first couple of days I ate normally but by the third I began to feel sick and started taking the Zofran, the nausea medication, the best kind you can get.

Now I lie in bed, day after day, simply trying not to throw up. This is extremely boring but I don't dare to get up and move around. Even going to the bathroom is risky.

I know that I have to drink, and Don keeps a glass of ginger ale on my night table, which I sip as often as I can, a major task. I use it to force down the capsules of Temodar and the welcome Zofran.

This is supposed to happen one week every month for six months. Knowing that I will be visiting the shoals of illness every three weeks fills me with dread and unwilling submission, which nobody can take away from me if I want to live.

PART FIVE

HIGH SOCIETY

I DIDN'T MEAN TO SAY THAT

When I open to door to let Marnie and Patty in, the aroma of savory roast chicken and vegetables with herbs wafts in. They have brought lunch. This is one of the weeks I'm not taking Temodar and have some appetite, enough for me to take several forkfuls of the heavenly dish.

I don't know Marnie and Patty well, but I like seeing them at the Unitarian church and at Pema's weekly meditation and reading.

I put the leftovers in the refrigerator as they settle on the couch, then go over to join them. "Excuse, but speech worse getting. Radiation and chemo."

"My new book about reincarnation is coming out soon," Patty offers. "It follows one soul through several bodies. I'll give you a copy when it comes out."

"I'm going to a great birding trip to Ohio on May 5th, during the migration." Marnie says, anticipation in her voice. "There are 37 species of warblers there!"

"What did you think about the sermon the guest speaker gave on Sunday?" Patty wonders. "It sounded a little like Unity Church."

I went once to Unity Church and was not impressed. They believe in healing through prayer; I went briefly during a bad spell with MS. Once my prayers seemed to be answered, but not on the next two times. That was no greater than chance, my scientific standard.

"Oh, the them…iti idiots," I scoff.

Both women sit bolt upright with expressions of shock.

"I used to go there," Patty chokes out. "I learned a lot there when I first got started writing books."

Why is it exactly that I'm trying to talk?

KWANZAN MOVING FLOWERS

Sometimes I just lie on the couch under a black and gold quilt, looking out on the cherry tree in the back yard. I need to rest a lot, maybe only being able to do one thing before needing a break.

We planted this tree, a Kwanzan cherry, when we moved into this house in January 2000. The tree was then a tiny, scraggly bush-like thing, looking as if it would blow away in a light breeze. Now it reaches past the roof of our two-story house, and its branches spread out to fill the back yard.

As it does every April, the cherry tree is beginning to flower. Several flowers have started to open. This is one of the frequent times I just stay still, not thinking but simply watching things around me or listening to the ambient sounds.

I have never looked at this tree in this way before. This time I observe that these blooms are opening very quickly, so at one point I see one of them with a tight pink bud looking closed but the base of a flower appearing when I look at it again in an hour.

I lie here for hours, watching petals emerge and open, buds arriving on the branches, even leaves' green, sharp points just poking out.

There are branches on which buds have not yet appeared. They shall arrive in the coming days, and I shall watch them.

CAT TOOTH FOOD

My voice is worse today, but Salem needs food. Salem is generally a very healthy cat, but from an early age she has had bad teeth.

"Her teeth are worse than a ten-year old cat's," her vet had said, when Salem was two years old. "She has tartar all over everywhere, a rotten tooth, and even an infected area of gum. She really needs surgery."

A thousand dollars later, Salem was crouching under the bed, traumatized, refusing to take anything but a few laps of mashed-up wet food. I had to haul her out twice a day to give her antibiotic drops, which she usually spat out. This went on for a week.

It happened two more times.

At her last checkup, Dr. Fluke mentioned a new food, Science Diet Adult Oral Care. We have been giving it to Salem ever since and she has had no more pocketbook-busting, agonizing dental surgeries.

Today, I am in Pet Smart to buy her a new bag; Don needs to wait in the car to catch up with e-mails from his office. This is a new Pet Smart and I'm looking in the cat department, passing by feather toys and kitty condos.

A man in a red Pet Smart apron comes up.

"May I help you?"

"Tooth food," I say.

"What?"

"Tooth food," I repeat.

He recovers and asks "What is the name of the product?"

I shake my head no. I knew the name when I came in, but I can't remember it now.

"Okay, this is for a cat, right?"

"Cat," I confirm.

He leads me to an extensive array of canned and bagged cat food.

"Dry or wet?"

"Bag."

This still leaves a lot of choices.

"Okay, does the cat have bad teeth?" he tries.

"Yes."

The man looks over all the bags until his eyes light up.

"Is this it?" he asks, excited.

It is. Science Diet Adult Oral Care.

I can say "Thanks." And I triumphantly pick up the food.

HEISENBERG AT THE TABLE

We are in Dr. Arthur's office because my speech has taken a turn for the worse. Dr. Arthur is absent, so her PA, Dennis, is substituting for her.

I say "Speech sad mad bad." And then I ask, "Why?"

"That's just from the radiation, which can warp brain structures."

"What? Nobody told us about that. WARP?" Don squawked.

"Yeah, sure, it's ionizing radiation so it can happen, and it's usually permanent so you're unlikely to get better with the speech. Didn't the doctor at the radiation facility tell you? Of course, the Temodar is also making it temporarily worse, but basically the radiation's impact is likely to persist."

Don and I look at each other in horror.

"Are you sure?" Don chokes out.

"I'm really sorry, but that might be the way it goes."

Dennis is usually so much fun, always making wry jokes, so cultured that he has a lot to say about the museums and films he goes to. I know he's not being mean at all now, but I feel angry at him anyway.

On the way home, I feel tears start running down my cheeks.

"Do you believe him?" Don asks.

I just sit.

"Well," he goes on, "Dennis the Dour is full of crap. You're god damned GOING to get better! I'm going to personally make sure that you get better."

Don is the most optimistic person I know and he is usually right. I think about what he said, though, and wonder. I don't contradict him, just sit still, uncertainty washing through me. I don't know, and I'm getting really tired of things we don't know.

It would help me to develop a more adaptive response to the specter of uncertainty.

In 1927, the German physicist Werner Heisenberg derived the Uncertainty Principle, in which he showed that it is impossible to simultaneously determine the position and the speed of a particle. (Indeed, as modern physicist Hans Christian von Baeyer points out, since the particle has no position or speed before you observe it; "they are undefined, like the color of hope, the weight of joy, and the circumference of fear.")

This is the most basic statement of uncertainty and ultimately leads to the realization that there is no way for us to know whether my speech will improve or not.

There is no way to get away from Heisenberg. You might as well invite him into your house and welcome him to share your supper.

NICER

Ayya's sangha is a haven for me. We gather on Saturday afternoons, meditate, have a tea break, then settle down again for a teaching from Buddhist scriptures or a talk. The stillness is good for me.

Everyone is gathering, quieting down, settling on their cushions. Ayya's giant, prodigiously furry cat ambles past and curls up in his place, next to her pillow.

This a particularly bad brain day. When she walks by I ask "Remember how…before? It was…nice. Nicer. Do? You?"

"I don't understand," she answers sadly. "I feel terrible for you. You've been making words but they don't seem to mean what you want them to."

"Nicer!" I say vehemently and point to the ceiling where the air comes in.

"Something about the air? Do you want me to change something?"

I raise my hands and arms up high and sweep them down to my thighs.

"Oh, of course—do you want me to turn the air conditioner lower?"

"Yes yes!" I sigh in relief.

She makes a quick adjustment, sits down, rings the bell, and the peace of meditation takes over.

During the tea break, I sip on something flavored with ginger and listen to people talking, especially enjoying one person's account of her volunteer work with endangered animals. Her accounts of population counting methods make it unnecessary for me to talk.

"It's easier with pandas, they don't move around much," someone suggests.

"You'd be surprised—they hide!"

The bell for regathering rings and we forget about pandas.

The teaching is about the Eightfold Path, a guide to ethical living, including practices such as Right Speech, Right Thought, and Right Action. Ayya has presented these several times, but she manages to bring something new up every time.

"How long does it take to master the Eightfold Way?" someone asks.

"It depends on how hard you work on it," Ayya answers. Everyone laughs.

The afternoon draws to a close; people pick up their things and wander away. Don pulls into the driveway to pick me up.

"Nicer now?" Ayya asks after the session is over, as I'm on my way out.

"Nicer!" I give her a thumbs up.

PART SIX

SORROWS

THE VALLEY

One morning the phone rings; Don picks it up and hands it to me.

"Your father," he says. "He sounds upset."

Dad and I have, as we had agreed, had frequent phone calls. Don says that I can speak better when I'm on the phone, though neither he, I, or the doctor have any idea how this is possible.

"Hi, Dad, how you?"

"I'll tell you what's up," he says angrily. "I'm going to die. Soon. My chemo gave me pneumonia, so they won't give me any more, and my blood counts are a big mess."

I don't know what to say, and the reason is not aphasia. I truly just don't know what I can say that would help. There is no help.

"Sorry, so sorry," I try.

"I can finish my part of the paper by tomorrow so Jimmy can give it at the conference, but I'm going to miss it," he goes on in a disgusted tone.

At 93, an engineer, he and his research partner, Jimmy, are interested in the electrical aspects of running paper mills. He officially "retired" at a ceremony on his 65th birthday, according to his company's rules, but he began a new job as a consultant the next day. When that job eventually ended, he became a free-lance consultant, and has plenty of work, being especially in demand because he is the only person who knows how to fix some of the older equipment.

"Retirement is death," he had said on his 65th birthday. "Picasso and Segovia worked into their nineties, why can't I?"

He's attained his goal, but his blood cancer, multiple myeloma, is not going to let him go any further.

"I'll miss you, kid," he sighs.

"I love you," I tell him.

The last conversation with my father ends in an inadequate word, not because I can't say the word, but because the word itself is inadequate to lead him through the Valley of Death.

ANIMAL LOVERS FOREVER

"Meredith, Dad is sleeping and we can't wake him up. We have hospice-at-home, so he's not suffering, but he may not have more than a day or so," my sister, Maria, says on the phone.

"Does he wake?"

"No, but we think he is able to understand us," she explains, adding that "Robert (our brother) thinks so, too."

"How?" I ask.

"He squeezes our hands. I know you have trouble talking, but you do pretty well on the phone. Can you say anything?"

"Try," I offer.

"Okay, I'm putting the phone next to his ear."

What do I want to say? Can I say it? I think of him letting me ride on his horse in front of him, taking care of a sick puppy, showing me how to trim a cat's claws without making it cry. He had once promised me he would tell me about each horse he ever had. Too late for that, but the offer showed how much he had cared for them. My life has always included animals, and I know that his nurturing my own devotion to them in me is his legacy.

"Animals," I start. Giving myself a little time to think between words has sometime helps. "You … love … animals," I start, pausing a little. Then "I … love … animals."

I can hear him breathing.

"You, you, taught … me. Taught me. Taught me … love animals. Thank … you."

Maria is back on the phone.

"That was perfect! How did you think of that? He definitely heard you. He squeezed my hand really hard," she tells me.

My reply is a sob.

SILENT TEARS

My grandmother, my father's mother, had a stroke when she was 93 which left her with the ability to hear and understand speech, but not to speak herself.

I identify now with her now. She was so articulate, capable of long, creative, and intelligent conversations. Before she married my grandfather at 40, she was a professor of calculus and Latin. She home-schooled my father and uncle up until high school.

When we were little, she told us stories, wildly imaginative fairy tales, which our mother disapproved of because she thought they were scary and violent. (They never did us any harm.) In junior high school, I took Latin classes and Grandmother Ruth frequently explained complicated verb tenses, vocabulary, and the array of personal pronouns. As I became a teenager, she often told me things about how to get along with people and how to talk to boys.

She was the equal to Grandaddy Dixon (Dixon Lanier Merritt), who, while running a homestead in the country, was a newspaper editor and author of several books. He also authored a long series of limericks about animals. One has become a classic: "The Pelican," about a bird whose beak can hold more than its belly can.

Dinner conversations were far-ranging and full of good stories, such as the sighting of a fox with cubs: where he saw them, what they were doing, how many cubs there were.

He had a sharp edge, though, and would deliver a stern lecture if anyone made an error in grammar or syntax, and sometime made us feel like we were in a spelling bee.

"Meredith, how you spell "giraffe"? he asked one night.

"G I R A F E," I said.

"No! Incorrect! It has two 'f's."

My grandmother jumped in, asking "Did you know that each giraffe its own different patterns of spots? And that they eat the leaves of acacia trees, which happen to be the exact right height for a giraffe's head?"

Her words saved me from a very sticky wicket.

I was 20 when she had her stroke, which was the same affliction that Grandaddy Dixon had succumbed to a couple of years earlier. My father asked me if I would like to ride up with him to see her in her nursing home, which was in the small town of Darien Center, in upstate New York, where our people on that side come from.

When we got there the nurse said "Right before the stroke, Ruth was having a conversation in Latin with her roommate, another former teacher. But suddenly she was not able to speak at all. She can hear perfectly and she's been very upset."

My grandmother looked at us in dismay. We talked to her, simply saying that we loved her. She wanted to say something but tears ran copiously down her still beautiful face, high cheekbones, sea-green eyes. Her brilliant smile was gone, though; her full lips were open as she labored to get hold of a word.

I cry her tears now.

STANLEY YATES MERRITT
1926-2019

My father has died, on May 9. Maria tells me this around noon.

"He was clinging so hard," she says. "Finally I told him it was okay to let go."

Don picks up on the other handset.

"Maria, I'm sorry," he tells her.

"It was time," she replies. "The funeral is in two weeks, but I know Meredith probably can't travel."

"No, I don't think so," Don says.

"Well, I have a lot of calls to make, so I'd better go. I just wanted you know first."

My Dad. He was a study in contradictions, sometimes as harsh as his father was to him, but more often kind and compassionate, quick to anger but so quick to forgive.

Starting out as a proponent of punishment, he later decreed that there would be no more spankings.

Stern at first in response to my getting a failing grade in Algebra, he took pity on me when I flung the textbook, denting the wall, and, when I told him the subject was like a foreign language, started at the beginning and taught me the baby steps.

I have too many memories to easily record, but the one I treasure most is the cycle of stories he spun for us when we were small, about the adventure of a fox couple, Vulp and Vixen, and their cubs. Vulp and Vixen took the cubs to the top of the mountain to slide down the snowy peak. They went fishing by a pool at the bottom of a waterfall. The pair and their younglings ran through the forest half the night to meet up with their fox cousins in a moonlit clearing.

Granddaddy Dixon had told Dad fox stories too; you could hear the foxes' raspy, sharp barking on the farm site and the topic was a natural one. I mistakenly thought Dad had been retelling those stories to us.

When I asked him if he could tell them to me so I could write them down, he chuckled. "No, I made those stories up. When I asked if I could write his down for you kids, he said 'No, son, it doesn't work that way. You have to go to the fox yourself to get your own stories.'"

What fox he talked to I don't know, but his answer sent me on my own path. I found a pair of foxes, an adolescent, and one young cub who came out into a nearby field at dusk. The dog fox, the male, came up to me and barked; I barked back, and we had a conversation, until he accepted me and walked back into the field. The foxes became comfortable with me and let me watch them forage for prey, the vixen sometimes prancing in the movements known as "charming" mice.

I did a series of paintings of foxes. One of these, a painted hexagonal drum showing three foxes, without eyes, flying around a half moon, has been in a museum show.

I have no children to tell the stories to, but people have seen my foxes.

Now, since MS has crippled my hands and brain surgery has left something missing in my imagination, unable to paint, I look back on that eldritch picture and realize that I am the last in a line of fox shamans.

NOT YOU

There is a loud rapping at the front door.

Sandy is standing there, wiping tears off her face.

I motion for her to come in and lead her to the couch, sitting next to her, arm around her shoulders.

She sobs, not saying anything.

"What?" I ask her.

"Ellie," she chokes out. "Ellie died."

"How?"

"Nobody knows, Joe just came home last night and found her collapsed on the floor."

Two days ago, my father; today, Ellie. Heaviness settles over me, and Sandy and I weep together.

After a while, she says "I shouldn't have said it."

"What?"

"I told her she was too fat, that it would cause her to have a heart attack, that she should quit eating dessert and eat more vegetables. She was sort of mad at me, and that was our last conversation."

Ellie was 50 and had a number of illnesses, most notably something that resembled lupus. She may have had a heart attack, but there were other possibilities. She also seemed depressed and I briefly entertain the notion that she may actually have taken her own life. I hope not.

Sandy is thinking the same thing.

"If she killed herself it's my fault," Sandy moans. "I was just trying to get her to take better care of herself."

"Not you."

"I hope not."

We sit silently until she stood up and "Okay, I can't do anything about it. Maybe she did have a heart attack. It wasn't me."

I hold her hand as she walks toward the door and goes out onto the porch.

"Not me," she repeats.

"Not you."

MY RABBIT

The women of the Unitarian church are all wearing hats, with feathers, jewels, ribbons, and yes, sequins, at Ellie's funeral in tribute to Ellie's penchant for *chapeaux*. The men's heads look quite bare.

The church is packed. Everybody loved Ellie.

Sandy sits next to me, snuffling.

Anna Jo closes her eulogy by saying "We will never have another Ellie."

I eat too many deviled eggs while composing what to say to Joe in my mind. This is something I have found useful, plotting words ahead of time and reciting them over and over to myself, so I can speak somewhat understandably. Ayya says this makes me sound like a schoolmarm.

It turns out to be unnecessary, as Joe himself is totally incoherent.

"I don't know how, I just don't know…" he mumbles. He is still in shock.

Cindy comes up, holding a large cardboard box full of tissue-wrapped objects.

"I gathered up Ellie's miniature rabbits and hares, so everyone can have one," she explains. "Here's one I think you'll like."

Ellie had two pet rabbits, known as Rupert and Honey-Bunny, who she let run around the house and lie on the couch. She was so fond of lagomorphs that she amassed an astonishing number of rabbit and hare figurines, with which she filled two big glass display cases.

My rabbit is black and white and crouches in a small ball on a grass-green oval base. Her ears prick up but her head is held low, so that her ruby eyes barely show. She looks so innocent and vulnerable.

PEAKS OF OTTER

"Dad's."

"What?" Don asks, puzzled.

"Funeral."

"Yeah, Maria said it would be day after tomorrow."

"Can we?"

Don shakes his head firmly. "No. You're not well enough."

I sit there, wiping tears away.

"Hmm. You really miss your Dad."

I nod and reach for a Kleenex.

He relents. "Okay. We'll go up tomorrow if we can get a room at the Lodge. The other hotels are God-awful."

The Peaks of Otter Lodge is right off the Blue Ridge Parkway, nestled in the mountains, and has a view of a crystalline lake from which you can see Flat Top and Sharp Top, both popular locations for hiking.

"Really? You have a room? Great. Could we stay tomorrow night?" I hear Don say to the receptionist.

Yes! We can go!

We drive up the slow way, up the winding Parkway itself, rather than using the highways. The forests are tenderly and achingly beautiful, the emerging leaves a delicate green and the birds winging from place to place.

My hands have been shaking, but in the excitement I manage to hide it.

The summer crowds have not yet come, and we easily find a table in the usually packed dining room, choosing one right by the lake. It seems chilly, so we put our sweaters on.

The waiter comes up to the table without menus.

"Sorry, folks, the power's off, so we just have some sandwiches we've been keeping in a cooler. Do you want a couple of them?

Well, it's too late to go into Roanoke to another place, so cold sandwiches it is.

The room is freezing and we put on layers of clothing, pulling the one inadequate blanket over us. Shivering, I wonder if I will be able to sleep at all.

But soon I become tired, so tired. Sleep comes amazingly quickly, sucking me under a black stream. Deep, deep sleep, irresistible. I surrender.

WELCOME TO THE DUST BIN

How long have I been asleep this time? By now I know this is another toxic interaction and that I have been hospitalized. I see Don sitting on a chair facing the door; the wall seems to be triangular. This is not a normal room.

"Hey, Don." He turns to me, awkwardly sideways.

"Where?" I ask. I wonder if we're still in Virginia.

"Charlotte. You weren't conscious this morning and I carried you to the car. Maria met us as we were leaving and said I should take you to the Bedford hospital, but we had a bad experience there before. I wanted you take you where we could talk to your regular doctors. I just got on the Interstate and hauled ass."

So I had missed my own father's funeral after all.

I sneeze, feeling assailed by dust; my eyes itch as if there was sand in them.

A nurse comes in, holding vials for blood, and Don excuses himself to go home and rest after the four-hour drive.

"We've been titrating your blood since you got here. You seem to have several toxicities so it might take a couple of days to get it sorted out," the nurse explains.

Great. I really feel like another hospital experience.

I have to go to the bathroom and know better than to set off the flashing lights and klaxon sounds the bed is wired with to announce that a patient with poor balance is up. I would provoke pandemonium if I stood up and stepped forward. Once a fall risk, always a fall risk. I push the button and wait.

Eventually, a plump man with interesting braids comes in to assist me. He looks like he might be good humored.

When I went in, a noxious odor nearly bowls me over. I come out joking "Cat pee," holding my nose.

The guy, Rodney, checks it out.

"Oh maaan," he grumbles, pulling out a laundry bag full of dirty linens. "And I even liked that cat!"

SENESCENCE

The night after I was in the hospital, I was brooding about missing my father's funeral. I could not sleep at all.

Compounding my preoccupation, a nurse comes in about every hour to check my temperature, blood pressure, and heart rate. At least this one has stories to tell me.

"I'm working at another hospital in the morning. I don't get to sleep until evening because I'm bringing my family from India, from Calcutta. One family member at a time."

"Interesting family," I say. She goes away after making her notes on my chart. Now I can't sleep because I find this woman interesting.

In an hour she's back. "What's wrong with you?" she asks.

Of course I can't say metabolic encephalopathy, so I just say "Brain."

"Does your head hurt?"

"No," I say. "But tell more me, Calcutta."

She goes on about each member of her family who has already come, and then she has to leave again.

When she returns, she tells me who is still planning to come. "How many?" I wonder.

"Ten," she says. I'm amazed.

After she leaves, I slip to sleep after all, the light beginning to rise.

I am unpleasantly awakened by the sound of voices. Now I get to sleep? Not fair.

It turns out to be a doctor I don't know, talking with Don. I have to wake up for them.

The doctor enthusiastically says, "I figured the problem out. You have to stop taking all of your neurological and psychological medications, except half your dose of risperidone, because the consequences of suspending that are too serious. Everything that affects your brain can interfere with brain function and can cause encephalopathy now that you're over 60."

"Really?" says Don. "That's interesting—why is it like that?"

"It's the metabolism," the doctor says. My heart sinks. All of them? I wonder.

No more MS medication? Decimated bipolar medication? What is going to happen to me?

FALLING STAR

I'm still awake. It's five in the morning, and I haven't slept at all.

Should I try to go to church? Why not? I'm so wired I'm clearly not going to get any sleep. Silently, so as not to wake Don, I dress and go downstairs, make coffee, and wait for him, and fidget.

He comes down late, finishing off the coffee.

It seems that everything I say irritates him. In fact, it's the other way around.

I ask him if he would take the trash out.

"Can't it wait? It's Sunday, tomorrow will be fine."

"Why are you using THAT TONE?"

Bewildered, he says "I'm not using any tone."

I begin to cry. "I'm sorry. I'm so rude."

"Look, are you sure you're up to going to church?"

I nod through my tears.

On the way, I cry. When he pulls up to the porch to let me out, he asks the same thing. I nod again.

I try not to talk to anyone, but the minister comes over and says "Let me know if there is anything I can do to help you."

There isn't. During the service, I get control, and by the time

149

Don comes back to pick me up, I feel great. In fact, I think it would be fun to go to the NC Zoo.

"The Zoo? Why? You're not even well enough for us to get that far! What's wrong with you today?"

I sulk the rest of the afternoon. It would be so great to see the baboons and their antics.

Early dinner, early bedtime.

Again, I can't sleep, so I go down to the living room.

I don't even turn the lights on. Sitting on the couch, looking out the window even though I can't see anything, I weep again, for hours, perceiving nothing but futility and absence of hope.

DOWN-A-DAY A-DOWN A-HEY

The refrain of a song is running through my head, surely from listening to Peter, Paul, & Mary when I was a kid. I'm trying to recall the title of the song. I know the music but am not sure. It may have been "The Three Ravens", an old ballad about murderous birds plotting their crimes.

Yes…it comes back to me now.

> "Three ravens sat upon a tree
> With a hey a derry down derry down
> They were black as they might be
> With a down a hey
> One of them said to its mate
> "What shall we for our breakfast take?
> With a down a hey a derry derry down…"

The song is melancholy, doleful, hypnotic. That's me. A black bird might eat me up.

When we refer to being "down", it makes sense, just as does its opposite, "I'm on top of the world." This applies to emotions in normal proportions. Unless you have had clinical depression, "down" just means that you're not in a good mood.

But if you have been there yourself, you can truly understand how apt the analogy is.

Down. All the way down the well, at the bottom of the hill, in the dumps.

So far down you can't imagine how to get back. It isn't possible to even reach up.

I wish I still had the vinyl LP and turntable of that time and could listen to someone singing "The Three Ravens" as tunefully as Peter, Paul & Mary, rather than playing it over and over in my mind.

MIDNIGHT BEAK

I jump when the phone rings. I jump when almost anything startles me. It's Dr. Simmons.

"Hi, Meredith. Juanita says you're having some trouble."

"Bad sleep, bad mood."

He sighs. He has taken away all my medications and now I'm in a bad way.

"You have bipolar symptoms and you need risperidone, but I'm afraid to give you very much since you had a toxic reaction to it. How about a low dose?"

"Fine."

"Ok, I'll call in a small amount, and restart lithium," with a warning to let him know if I have any untoward symptoms. I am not hopeful about the small dose of risperidone.

The next day I am not bothering with dressing, taking a shower, or having breakfast, just thinking about the ravens in the song I was obsessing about last night.

When I'm bipolar, I can write poetry. I haven't published any, because I can only do it when I'm on the outer edge of melancholy with the flux of irrational words flooding my mind, not when modern medicine returns me quickly back to normal.

153

I read a book by Kay Redfield Jamison called "Touched by Fire," about poets who were manic-depressive and probably could not have written as brilliantly as they did if drugs like risperidone had been invented.

Edgar Allan Poe is one of the best-known American poets who was manic-depressive, and his phrase "Quoth the raven 'Never-more" brings home the raven as a symbols of death.

Sitting at my keyboard, I brood, then type "Birds of Prey," and finally write:

> The golden owls that fly between the worlds
> On swift, soundless wings;
> Ravens dark as night perching on trees,
> Looking, looking, with sharp black eyes;
> These are the birds that bring us to our death,
> Without our knowing when, or where, or why.
> I think a raven is searching for me,
> And when he snatches me up in his midnight beak,
> I know he will fly and fly and fly.

I could be famous if I were willing to live with being crazy.

REPEAT AFTER ME

My nightmare, of being captured by an evil doctor who wants to perform painful tests on me, wakes me up with horror and fear. I am trembling, in a state of panic.

The small dose of risperidone is not working, so I call Juanita at Dr. Simmons' office and have to leave a message. Juanita always says she has problems understanding me, a problem she had even before I had language issues. But today, I feel that nobody should have difficulty understanding what I say.

"I had a nightmare in which some doctor captured me and threatened me with painful tests. I'm very upset and I think Dr. Simmons should give me a higher dose of risperidone."

Don sat right next to me and said that the message was perfectly understandable.

When Juanita called back she said "So you had a dream. I didn't understand what it was about. But Dr. Simmons says you should take one risperidone in the morning and two at night, what you were taking before you were in the hospital."

"Good," I said. "I'm sure that will help."

"Now do you remember how you're going to take them?"

"One in the morning, two at night." She is treating me as if I were a small child.

"Yeess, that's right! One in the morning and two at night!" She treats me like a small idiot child!

I have a flash of insight. Maybe I annoy her as much as she annoys me. I decide to try something new.

"Juanita, sorry talking to you like kid. Should talk to you grown-up."

"I know," she laughs. "Don't worry about it, honey. I deal with all kinds, but thank you for admitting it."

FUNERALS

Something is seriously wrong. My speech is almost delirious. Don can barely understand what I'm trying to say. I have to make an appointment with Dr. Simmons, and we're not sure he will deal with us or refer it to Dr. Arthur.

"Let's go see him," Don says, "maybe he can help because the last time this happened it was a medication problem."

When we arrive at the office Dr. Simmons greets us with his usual smile, but I shake my head almost angrily.

"I can't…I can't…" I try to say.

Dr. Simmons says, frowning with worry on his face, "Come on in, I can tell we need to look at this right away. What's going on?"

"I am trying talking call can't talk words not coming out silly Billy Willy you know what I mean I don't know I don't know I don't know what what," I go on. Dr. Simmons looks even more worried.

"Has she been lucid at all today?" he asks Don.

"No, I can't get any sense out of her," Don says. Dr. Simmons gets out my chart and starts looking over it.

Shaking his head, he says, "This is the same thing we have seen several times, but it seems like something else is different. Could be brain, MS, the usual list of suspects. I see that your lithium level is up again, so cut it in half."

Suddenly I began to cry, covering my face, breaking down. He just waits for me to calm down.

"Father father father died dad dead, gone away where is he how where can't go on." I vainly try to control my words, explain, my voice fading away. "And my my friend friend Ellie dead, too."

He says, "This happened last month, but it still seems like it's going on now. This speech pathology is also psychological, and has gotten worse." He looks at me with infinite sympathy, sitting silently for a while.

"Funerals," I mumble.

"Grief," he says, "grief could be making this so much worse. "Your thoughts are disordered, but your feelings are so much more important here."

He just looks at me and I look at him, ending the session without any further discussion, just opening the door and placing his hand on my shoulder.

PART SEVEN

HASTEN SLOWLY

BOY COY TOY

"Where Salem's coy boy toy so play can? Her play with cat cat I her er toy need, feathers," I call out to Don. "Feathery on stick. Dangle it dangle it down jumping."

Despite my difficulty, Salem sees the feathered stick, springs up to action and proceeds to cavort and twist in the air for several minutes before finally flopping over onto her side.

How can I manage to talk with other people like this? I wonder. I reflect on this, knowing I have to make do with this flapping for the duration. I don't know how long I will have to keep this up, but damned if I will babble all the time. I need to use the TS, telegraphic speech, that Anya told me would prove valuable. I've not been using it consistently.

I sit and ponder this, knowing it will be a long effort. I feel desolate with three months remaining until I finish chemotherapy, and until I will have a chance to start speech therapy. Dr. Arthur has just warned me this will be the most difficult part of my treatment, with increasing nausea, exhaustion, and sleepiness from the Zofran, the powerful nausea medicine.

I know that little can happen as this time passes. I just have to continue being patient, patient, and more patient. I have little to say to myself except that I will get through it the way I have gotten along so far, even managing this effort during the boring months ahead.

My afternoon begins to wane, as familiar sleep quickly approaches. I drag myself onto the couch, struggling with the familiar sinking feeling which seems to keep me from doing anything substantive. Stubbornly I try to stay awake and succeed for once.

Faith, hope, and perseverance. These are all I have in my arsenal at this point, and I must make do with them.

DARK SHADOWS

We have been watching a 60s show called Dark Shadows, about the life of Barnabas Collins, a vampire. He lives in a town near Bangor, Maine, his lifetime spanning the 18th, 19th, and 20th centuries. His story is about his ongoing quest to avoid being discovered, his family life with a large cast of characters, and his continuous involvement with the supernatural.

His nemesis is the witch Angelique, he met in Martinique, who curses Barnabas because he spurns her love, earning her permanent hatred and desire to make him miserable. She eventually causes his beloved fiancée to commit suicide, and spends the rest of time keeping him from falling in love with anyone else.

At this point in the story, she has enlisted the services of Ben Stokes, a convict who is condemned to work for Barnabas. Ben has learned about Angelique's plot and wants to reveal it. As he begins to speak to Angelique, she casts a spell on him, enjoining him from doing so, causing him to be unable to speak at all if he tries.

I sympathized with his struggle to force words out of his mouth, thinking of my own difficulty with that process.

I am following the plot pretty well, when a new element

is introduced. The fiancée, Josette, puts on a cologne that Angelique has set out for her, causing her to entice Barnabas' brother Jeremiah. She makes an advance on him and is ashamed, crying hard and running upstairs to her room. Jeremiah is shocked.

My chemo fog is making me a little fuzzy, and I ask "Who was that man she was with?"

Don looks at me in surprise and says it says that it was Jeremiah.

All right I say. My mind kind of wandered.

Next a box arrives for Josette, which isn't expected and leads to confusion about where it came from, whereupon she comes down from her room. They cautiously unwrap the gift, discovering that a skull, newly severed, falls suddenly to the floor and rolls, terrifying both.

I am getting sleepy and yet again ask something.

"Who sent the skull?"

"We don't know," Don answers. "They haven't shown us yet."

I just drift off, feeling deprived of the knowledge. I have to let go of the concern, accepting that I may not find out. This is something of a lonely feeling, my communication leaving me. I fall to sleep with a lingering sense of desolation.

IT'S ALL IN YOUR HEAD

Veronica, Dr. Corbett's nurse, stands next to me with my chart.

"What's going on?" she asks.

"Thin," I answer. I use the smallest number of words possible now.

She looks at the chart.

"Oh, my, you only weigh 90 pounds! You're usually 110—what's wrong?"

"No food."

"Yes, I can see that you're on chemotherapy. I'll get Dr. Corbett."

Dr. Corbett isn't just any doctor. He knows everything, always smiles, takes his patients seriously and treats them as if they were personal friends. He makes jokes, good ones; he's just funny. He is so much fun that it makes being sick bearable.

"There needs to be more of you," he comments. "We call this cancer cachexia, meaning that your chemotherapy has suppressed your ability to maintain adequate nutrition," he starts. "I can give you some guidelines that might help."

He lists avoiding strong-smelling food, eating several small meals throughout the day, drinking Ensure, indulging in anything that sounds good, even dessert, and taking a vitamin and mineral supplement every day. He also wants me to take an appetite stimulant.

As he fills out the prescription, he looks at me with a crazy grin.

"How does this happen?" he bursts out, flinging his hands up in the air. "How does one person get three serious neurological diseases? MS, bipolar disorder, and now brain cancer! All your problems are literally in your head!"

PRAISE FOR THE FISH

I am hungry! Often, even when not nauseous, I feel not inclined to eat, but the appetite stimulant is beginning to work and today I am actually ready to enjoy a real meal.

"Hey that's great," Don rejoices. "Would you like to go to Red Rocks for lunch?"

"Yes."

Red Rocks is an American restaurant with a variety of classic dishes. We haven't been out to eat for quite a while and both of us are excited about the prospect. Like two children on an adventure, we collect ourselves and head for the car.

It's a bit of a ride to the next town, Huntersville, but the drive is pleasant. We take the back road, where there are beautiful old houses lining the streets. Between sections of houses, there are stretches of woods, which are now lush and green, and we do not hurry.

When we get to the small town of Huntersville, we head for Birkdale, a collection of shops, restaurants, apartment buildings, and a movie theater.

"Are you strong enough to walk down on the sidewalk for a few minutes?" asks Don. This does not go so well, so we abandon the idea and go straight to Red Rocks. Once seated, we work look at the menu, enjoying the long list of options.

"I want chicken penne. I know I always get it but it really is my favorite," Don confesses.

"Give me a little more time to make my mind up. There are some things I haven't even tried yet. Finally I decide that I want to have the Cajun salmon entrée, which comes with wild rice and a medley of steamed vegetables.

"That's a good choice," the waiter comments, as he scribbles down our orders.

While we wait, we look around at the array of art, abstract and landscapes. We especially like a painting, which shows red and blue blocks, with yellow crisscross patterns over these.

We are good and hungry by the time the waiter returns and lays our plates out. We taste we taste and compare notes.

"How is yours?" Don wonders, smiling at his penne. I have only taken a bite of mine, unable to speak because my mouth is full.

Don gobbles his dish, as he always does. I take my time, savoring each bite. He is used to sitting and watching me eat.

My vegetables come in a delectable lemon sauce, thoroughly crispy-black on the top with a creamy seasoning. I cut it up and mix it with the rice, pouring more Cajun flavored sauce. I fork bites up slowly, dragging out the melted flavors. This is the hungriest I've been in a long time, and I'm enjoying every bit of it.

"Do you want dessert?" asks Don. Now I am beginning to be a little stuffed and decide not to push my luck. He orders a slice of cherry pie, with a scoop of vanilla ice cream sprinkled with little black specks that comes with good vanilla. Now it is my turn to watch, and he again eats it quickly. This is a habit, and I will never understand why he doesn't sit still and savor his food. His loss.

By the time the check comes, I am beginning to feel tired and want to go home. I feel thankful for the meal. Some indigenous peoples thank the animal they are eating to honor its spirit. I give thanks to this salmon most gratefully.

NEW POTATOES

Today my new speech therapist is coming. Dr. Corbett had agreed to refer me to a private agency because Dr. Arthur said she didn't think I was ready. Dr. Corbett was dubious and said I might not have much luck, but give it a try anyway.

This will be my second therapist. Since Anya was here I have lost a good bit of what she taught me. I wait anxiously on the couch, watching for the new therapist's car to pull in, hoping that she will be able to help me with the current problems I have been having with talking.

Before long she arrives, gets out of her car and walks up to the door. I open the front door and welcome her in.

"I'm Angie. I have to say something," she starts. "You are my hero, I mean, everything you have been through and you are still here hoping to improve. I will do anything I can to help you reach your goal." She pauses. "I have to also tell you that this is my first assignment and you are my first client. I hope I can do a a good job."

She sets her bag on the couch between us and pulls out a pad of paper, where she draws a picture of a clock and tells me to mark where the hands would be if I added 11 minutes. I take the pencil, put it on the clipboard she has handed me, and try to follow her instruction, only to find that I can't tell where the mark should fall. I take a stab at it but get only to about six minutes when I show her the clock. She frowns.

"Well," she says, "that's not quite right. Why don't you try another number like 25 minutes." By the time I have tried my pencil mark, it has blurred on the clock. It is sloppy and I am struggling to see where 25 minutes would fall. Angie takes the pencil and pad back and says we need to try another exercise. She takes out a pack of brightly printed cardboard cards, shuffles them, and pulls out pictures to make an array of four. Now she asks "What do you see?"

"Feet."

"Do you see different kinds of shoes?" she says, trying again.

I can see that there are tennis shoes, high heels, sandals, and boots, but I can only say "Feet."

Now Angie is beginning to look frustrated but tries pulling out a different game. This one looks even more complicated to me and it turns out to be a flip chart with pictures.

She says "Try to make a sentence. Put the pictures up next to the noun, verb, adjective, and another noun. I follow her instructions.

She doesn't seem to realize that this is even harder. She just seems desperate for me to do it right. Wildly I flip the pictures, putting a frog in front, someone hiding something, something new, and a vegetable.

I say "Amy, potatoes, hide, new."

Angie replies, "Why would anyone hide potatoes?"

Angie tells me that the words are in the wrong order, that it isn't a sentence anyone would use. She looks down and begins to snuffle, and she shakes her head. She says "I don't think I can do anything for you; there just isn't enough for me to work with."

Her first day! I take her hand and squeeze it, saying "It's OK, not your fault." She gathers her things, slowly, and moves towards the door, quietly closing it behind her. Now I begin to cry myself, I was her hero. Some hero! Anya never would have done this; she would have said she would come again to try. This girl is inexperienced and has no idea what she is doing. I just sit there, angry thoughts running through my head. Would I ever speak properly again?

My thoughts settle down and I realize that what I really feel is compassion. Poor thing, her very first day.

A WASTED AFTERNOON

The appetite stimulant is still working; I've gained two pounds and I have started to enjoy regular meals, at least during this three week period when I'm not taking Temodar.

"Would you be up to going to Maggione's?" Don suggests. "I could really go for lasagna and you could get eggplant Parmesan with a nice Caesar salad. Lots of calories."

Well, I'm hungry enough and am willing to give it a try.

Maggione's is adjacent to SouthPark Mall, about forty minutes away, and by the time we get there my stomach is rumbling. As we're walking toward the restaurant, I feel dizzy.

"Some something…uh terrible…" comes out and I sink to the ground. Don pulls me up quickly and I can stand, but my blood sugar is dangerously low and I need to eat as soon as possible.

A family is driving up on the parking deck. They stop, and a man jumps out of the car, yelling "Stop! Stop! I'm calling an ambulance! Get in your car and wait."

"No, don't, she's fine, just got light-headed. She needs to get something to eat," Don protests.

"I'm an intern and I saw you fall. It's my duty to get you to the hospital."

The ambulance appears, siren on, and the eager intern demands that Don follow the ambulance to go to the nearest hospital, giving directions. I'm indignant, but I am unceremoniously hustled into the vehicle on a stretcher by two burly paramedics, who enthusiastically try to start an IV. The driver pulls out, wheels squealing, siren blaring.

At the hospital, I am rushed into the emergency room. Don arrives, calling the officious intern a long string of highly derogatory names.

A doctor is hovering, noting my cancer on the records he pulls up, telling one nurse to order a CT scan, stat, and asking another to check my pulse, blood pressure, and temperature.

"These old people with cancer wandering around, they're a danger to themselves," the doctor grumbles. (I'm 65.)

To my perverse delight, the macho medics were not able to get a line for an IV.

"She has an IV port," Don explains. "You're not going to get anywhere without using it." The nurse scurries away to get somebody with the requisite skill set.

To the doctor, Don points out that my blood sugar is low and all I need is food. "Why don't you check her blood sugar? How about getting her some crackers or something?"

"We can't give her anything to eat or drink in case she needs surgery," the nurse fusses.

I am not allowed to go to the bathroom myself.

The doctor orders test after test, with long waits between results for each. Four hours have gone by and money is leaking out of our pockets.

Finally the doctor comes into the room with a clipboard holding the test results.

"I can't find anything wrong with you," he announces. "I guess you can go."

We could have told you that, I think, wishing that manners would let me say it.

"We, we might still be able to get dinner," Don says hopefully on the way out.

Maggione's has already closed.

LOSING THE TIMELESS

As I lie in the bed, I begin to think about the state of my meditation practice. I am feeling nauseated, but I can still concentrate a little bit.

I realize that, although I used to meditate every day, this has fallen off. Now I only do it at intervals, and find that I have trouble getting into the right state of mind. One needs to sit still, locating the body in space, becoming quiet, and consciously breathing in and out, eventually arriving at the state where you are not entertaining thoughts. If they come into your head, you are supposed to let them go. As I read in an instruction book for meditation, this is like inviting your thoughts in but not letting them stay. This should be pretty simple, but I seem unable to let the thoughts just dissipate. My mind is busy, and I don't settle down.

The infrequency of my meditation contributes to my inability to focus and be really quiet in my mind. Actually the idea is to at some point quit being based in the mind at all. It is important to be in the present moment without worrying about the past or projecting into the future. I need to find a way back to these practices. Daily meditation is the cornerstone of Buddhism, in order to develop equanimity, a sense of the timeless, and calm.

I haven't recently read any other Buddhist books or seen any of the YouTube entries put up by Ahjan Brahm. He mentions that the habit of checking to see when the meditation will finish, causes attention to turn to the future. This is what I have fallen into, unable to keep my mind on the practice and becoming bored. I always seem to do this.

Even though I have gone to Ayya Medhavi's sessions, I have let my practice go to pieces. I think it would be helpful to set a time for a phone conversation.

I call her and let her know the problem, in my best telegraphic speech.

"Of course," she says, "I'd be glad to talk to you about it."

I know she is not judgmental at all and is compassionate enough not to be upset with me. I need to wait until I finish this round of chemo before I can do anything that substantial, but we agree to put our heads together in a week and a half after the worst chemo, as the effects last four days after the administration of the actual medication, and I will not be well enough to have a serious conversation until then. But I am relieved that she will help me.

I decide it will be a good time to try meditating and following the guiding process she provides at her sessions. However, I can't settle down, thinking about the coming days, when I will be nauseated enough that I can't eat. My thoughts are too scattered; although one is supposed to eventually lose all sense of time, I have lost the timeless. I look forward to the time when Ayya Medhavi and I can address the issue.

THERAVADAN

It is 4 o'clock, the time I asked Ayya Medhavi, who runs the Charlotte Buddhist sangha, to call me, And I only have to wait for a few minutes. I know she is usually prompt and now the phone is ringing.

"Hi Meredith," she says. "How are you?"

"Well," I reply, "you know, having trouble with meditation. But how are you?"

"Actually, I am pretty good. I did not have a migraine today."

Ayya Medhavi has a terrible time with migraines, always having one pounding her head, so that she has had two consults with a neurologist about it. One of the doctors at my clinic has agreed to treat her without charge, being an unusually compassionate and highly ethical man. He hasn't been able to do much, however, and I know Ayya has a hard time.

She adheres, though, to the Buddhist first principal tenet, which she colloquially says is that suffering is inevitable, but pain is optional.

"Well," she says, "let's get to your concerns. I can't do more than one, you will just have to keep working on the other issues."

She proposes we start with the Eightfold Path. "I want to

emphasize the sixth section, which concerns the concept of Right Effort, which is not about working hard. It's about the need to work on any negative emotion or process that is interfering with your practice. What negative emotions do you think are most troublesome for you?"

I have to pause to think about that, and remember that last week I had an outburst about the presence of my anger and resentment at having such a serious illness, envying people who did not have to deal with such a thing. And I admit to myself that I have been struggling with some anger, which definitely gets in the way of calm practice. I convey this to her by simply saying "resentment and anger," and she knows what I mean.

"Well," she tells me, "it's not surprising. Those feelings are pretty normal, but how often do you have them?"

"Not often," I explain, "but enough." "And what do you do about it?" she inquires.

"Usually meditate, last week didn't work."

"Many people find that difficult," she says. "How does it feel when you are not experiencing those emotions?"

"Better," I explain.

"So you can rise above your baser instincts, and avoid unwholesome emotions. The concept of the unwholesome is really important, so you want to do and think things that will not drag you down."

"I agree. Be aware."

"I think you've got it. I hope you will use this lesson all the time and that you will find it rewarding." She closes the conversation, saying "I have a meeting in half an hour and I want to work a little bit on my presentation. I have to go, but I think this was a productive discussion."

"Me too, thanks, for go over this, real comfort."

With this she rings off. I will surely be able to avoid the negativity I was having last week, which I think should make me feel more settled. Most other people do not have to take chemotherapy pills for astrocytoma, but a lot of other people have other kinds of cancer. I will concentrate on compassion for them.

PEMA TARA

Pema, the second of the teachers I have asked to counsel me on meditation, said she would rather come to bring me some food and have a visit instead of having a phone conversation. Pema, being a lay practitioner, is not bound by the restrictions Ayya has. She is able to use her own car to meet, rather than relying on drivers to convey her.

Having trained in London and Boston, Pema has had decades of experience in teaching Tibetan Buddhism. It's a good thing that she has moved to Charlotte to live closer to her son and his children, since she brings a lively and informed presence.

When she arrives, she greets me warmly and brings in tubs of lunch food. She looks young for her age, even having streaks of black left in her hair. An avid vegetarian, she has learned to cook with accomplishment. Today she arrives with pasta made with what she calls fake meat and a crisp salad, accompanied by poppyseed dressing she has mixed.

"How are you?" she questions me. I never complain to her because she has such a positive outlook and always has a cheerful comment.

"Ok, how you doing?" I ask her in return.

185

"Very good," she answers. "I started a new group for the residents of my retirement home." Committed to a modest cost of living, she lives in a low-income residential complex. She has so many meditation groups I can't keep up with them.

Setting the table, Pema warms up the lunch dish and arranges plates, silverware, and salad bowls. Deftly she sets the meal out and we sit down. Of course, it is delicious and we don't say anything much as we dig in.

She mentions her recent retreat with the sage Tanzin Semtin, who has just given a session at the home of one of our members. A popular teacher, she is a little different from the usual. She is quick with a trenchant joke, responding to questions and getting right to the point. Her teachings are more pertinent to problems in peoples' lives and meditation practices than theoretical discourse. I have been to one of her sessions and hope to get to another one someday.

"Look," she says to someone, "you just have to accept that your husband is going to get along with his own issues, although it is up to you to maintain the compassion that you practice towards him, and things will go better. He will find something from your example."

Then she offers abounding love to a man who bursts out in grief and worry about his wife, who has been diagnosed with Alzheimer's and recently moved into an assisted living facility.

"Yes, you're losing your wife, your life together, feeling overwhelmed. I know you're trying to bring her as much quality of life to her as you can. This is a huge change and the impermanence is hard to take in." She rises and goes to him to give him a long, close embrace, as he weeps.

Pema washes the dishes and asks, "Now would you like to sit

in the living room and have a talk about your concerns with your meditation practice?"

We take mugs of steaming Himalayan tea and settle down on the couch, where I explain the problem.

"It sounds like you are having some trouble with concentration," she begins, "but you know already how to deal with that, just keep doing the best you can and it will come more easily."

"The most important thing for you to meditate on is not anything theoretical but simply the non-duality of the world. Remember that we are all One, and, although we tend to see things as separate, we are really the same part of the same universe."

"Yes," I agree. "This is best way. Happens sometimes spontaneously. Fills me with joy."

"Exactly," Pema replies. "For right now this is the most important thing you can include in your meditation. Over time it will become more and more accessible. Just remember that, and I think you will feel better. Do you have any other questions?"

"No, got it." We sit for a few minutes longer, relishing the early afternoon light streaming into the window. Pema says goodbye, holding onto my hands with warmth and tenderness.

"Thanks, thanks," I tell her, "so wonderful. Delicious food."

"Anytime," she says, as she closes the door. "You know I mean that."

I know this indeed, and I am awash with a sense of gratitude.

TIME'S ARROW

This is the last of my six one-week-per-month chemotherapy treatments. I have six days of this treatment to go, but after that I can forget about chemo. After so many treatments, the nausea has progressively gotten worse, but the end is in sight today. I have thrown up once and the next several days it may get worse, but I am overjoyed that it appears to have worked, along with the radiation earlier.

The first day of the six days, I don't feel well enough to stay out of bed but it is boring and I allow my mind to wander; today I pay attention to the passage of time, which sometimes drags and at other times jumps forward. I begin to wonder what time in fact really is; nobody seems to really know.

I remember conversations I had years ago with my physics professor in college about this topic. But now I can't yet read hard-core science beyond the simplest level.

I look up a couple things on my phone and retrieve and examine an explanation more suited to a simple level reader. Nowadays people are thinking of time in terms of the fact that we can make eggs into omelets but we can't make omelets into eggs, because time has passed. Once we can remember that the direction of time means that causes precede effects, and why we are born young and grow older. This is all because of entropy, which is the universal movement of order to disorder since the big bang occurred.

We experience the passage of time. Although we can speak of it in scientific terms, the truth is that it remains one of the most mysterious attributes of the universe, and we are the small ants who will never fully grasp it.

GOODBY AND HELLO

As I get ready for my last appointment with Dr. Arthur, I feel my heart lifting. I am too excited to say much on the way, but Don is waxing enthusiastic.

"Yes," he says, "you do have a lot on your plate to move on and get through speech therapy, and get your energy back, because you've been through so much."

We drive up to the Levine Cancer Institute complex, spend the usual amount of time cruising around the parking deck, going through the check-in routine, and then sitting for a long time waiting for Dr. Arthur. Today we wait for an hour, but since we are not waiting for bad news, it doesn't seem like such a long time.

Frances opens the door and waves for us to come in. Inside the room, Dr. Arthur is surrounded by her whole team, all smiling.

"You've finished your treatment!" she greets me. "Way to go! We'll have to follow you with screening MRIs every two months to make sure the tumor does not return, but I don't anticipate that."

"You too!" I want to tell her that she understands. "My part hard," I add.

"I am sure that's true," she tells me, "and I appreciate the effort you put in and the hard work by Don keeping you going. Now, since you have completed your radiation and chemotherapy, however, I don't want you to think it's all over now. It's going to take you quite a while to feel like yourself again and move into normal life. I encourage you to work your hardest to continue the fight, because it's not necessarily easy. Is there something that concerns you in particular?"

"Sure," I say; "chemo fog." I am wondering how long it will take before I am able to think as clearly as before.

She shakes her head, and observes that I may not be realistic, explaining that it can take up to six months.

"In fact, we often find that it is not productive to try speech therapy for six months."

"Six? Sooner. I will."

Everyone's expression ranges from pity to concern. Dennis in particular looks serious. There is a period of silence, during which I begin to shake, feeling overwhelmed by the prospect of another prolonged period of downtime.

"Do some people recover sooner than others? Is it variable?" Don wonders. Dr. Arthur says nothing yet.

But slowly she nods her head. "Yes, it is variable. You may recover soon but I didn't want to get your hopes up."

"Sooner for me," I declare. Her face is actually encouraging and she holds her hand to me as she says "it might be true, since you have gone so long so far."

We pack up and leave to the applause of everyone in the group.

"Thanks to all of you," Don says, as we return the happy looks.

On the way to the road we sit silent, and only when we get on the road I say, "Really you think?"

Don nods and says "yes, babe. You and I, we're going to keep working together as hard as we can to get you as normal as you can. I know it's not going to be all the way, I know there are things that will stick around, things you will always struggle with. But I can guarantee you are going to be talking within six months."

He reaches over, putting his hand on my knee, and says "Absolutely."

PART EIGHT

LOGOS

IT'S FINALLY TIME

Don and I are in the waiting room where I'll soon meet my new speech therapist. I beat Dr. Arthur's estimate by three months; the chemo fog has dissipated sooner than expected.

Don has his nose in his phone, but this time not answering emails from work. He's doing final edits on his forthcoming poetry collection, *Driving into the Dreamtime: New and Selected Poems*. He's won several awards for his poetry, and this will be his third published collection. Meanwhile, I am reading a children's book about cats.

"Meredith?" A woman, dressed in a black outfit printed with red poppies comes out. As I follow her, she introduces herself as Ashley, and I think that she is a woman who likes to dress for work. My jeans and sweater do not measure up, but we're not here to compare clothes.

I see that her office is small but neat, with a round wooden table in the middle and shelves filled with books to either side, along with a rack holding curious objects, some games obviously for children, puzzles, 3-D constructions, and some things I cannot identify.

"How are you?" she asks.

"Excited to start speech therapy," I say. "My third try."

"You know this is not going to be easy, and we will have to work very hard. You have to be aware of the fact that it may be frustrating. It says on your chart that you had a left temporal astrocytoma, and you may find yourself wanting to give up at times. Are you ready for this?"

She reaches down to a drawer in her desk and pulls out a sheaf of paper and three pencils. "This is the pretest I have to do in order to assess where are you are, and then we can set a plan."

I leaf through the folder and shudder at the sheer number of things I have to fill in. I see a section called paying attention and reading. I am supposed to find hidden letters M on a grid, and I have to match unfamiliar objects to a model, concentrating on detail. Then Ashley tells me she will tap after one minute.

Part 2 involves matching unfamiliar objects. Part 3 involves recalling numbers in a list, which is almost a total loss because I have dyscalcula, due to the fact that my tumor faced on my parietal lobe wiping out numerical manipulation. For Part 4, she shows pictures of objects so I can identify them, which also is tedious as I can see it will take me a while to call up the words.

Halfway through my eyes blur. "I'm getting pretty tired," I tell Ashley, and she says "Try to keep going; you only have two left to do."

Next, for Part 5, I have to complete sentences, and last, pick answers to questions about stories. I am surprised to see that this is not as difficult as I thought it would be, and finish the test on a positive note.

Ashley takes a few minutes to review the form, making a few notes. Then she looks up and smiles, saying "You didn't do too bad on that. I think I am going to classify you at a middle level."

The effort it took to take this seems worthwhile, and I am pleased to learn that I am not at rock bottom.

"We will start next week, working twice a week." She extends her hand and says "It is nice to meet you, and I think we will work well together. Stop at the desk and schedule next week's appointments."

Don looks up from his phone when I come out and asks "How did it go?"

"Better than I thought," I answer him. "Ashley says it will be hard work but can handle it."

"Let's go to P. F. Chang's for lunch. I think it's time for a reward."

SPOONS

Ashley greets me and introduces the topic of today's lesson: Spoons. I'm not sure I heard her right.

"Sorry? Did I hear spoons?"

"Yes, you did," she laughs. "We're going to talk about energy use, and I like to describe energy in terms of spoons."

This does not sound like speech therapy at all to me, and I don't know what to expect.

"You have trouble getting tired easily, right? Your speech is worse if you are worn out."

She's right about that; if I try to talk too long more gibberish will come out.

"Think of it this way," she explains. "You start each day with only a certain amount of energy, and it's important to ration energy during the day. Every time you use up a certain amount of energy, think of it as a spoonful of energy. You need to pause and rest for a little while."

This sounds kind of silly, but it does make sense.

"OK, do you want to do some work?" she asks. Of course I do, and I am pleased when she takes out an interesting looking pack of cards.

The first one she takes out is an animal, I think a giraffe. "Zebra," I say quickly, but then notice that the creature looks nothing like a striped horse. Why did I even say zebra? I feel foolish and correct myself.

"That was stupid," I say, shaking my head. "Of course giraffe."

"Your chart says that finding words is something you've had a lot of trouble with, so that you may see one thing and want to say something else, or even not be able to come up with the word at all. That's not anything to feel embarrassed about. It's just very common with a temporal lobe injury. Let's try again."

The next is a glass of water. I confidently say "cup."

"Close," Ashley encourages me. "Both a glass and a cup can hold water."

"I feel stupid," I say. "Right in front of me."

"Don't waste energy feeling stupid. You're not stupid, you have a hole in your brain, and anybody like you struggles with word recognition. Let's try just a few more."

The next few come more easily. I see and say "book, hat, and key." The first few mistakes must have been because I was nervous, I thought. Then I see a figure running. I see a person, but is it a boy, a girl, a man, or a woman? I stop and think, look carefully, and my answer, "girl," is correct.

She shows me a fish, and I produce the word fish, which I recognize quickly because I'm getting hungry.

Then she shows me a picture of something long and green and stringy. I had one of these at lunch yesterday, but what was it called? My face burns with frustration. Finally I have to give up. "I don't know."

"It's a stick of celery," Ashley fills in for me. "I think you're tired."

"Used up my spoons," I admit, sheepishly.

GAMES

Ashley has an interesting looking stack of pictures laid out for me today.

"I have some new games for you, but first tell me how you are doing with your spoons," she asks.

"Doing well," I answer her. "Slept late and had coffee and breakfast. Got dressed in something easy." Actually, this is the same thing I wore yesterday. No effort at all. I really want to get a lot done here.

"Good," Ashley approves, handing me the sheaf of papers. "The first page has three pictures. What do you see?"

"A clock, a shovel, and a toaster."

"OK, pick out the pictures which occur on page 1 from among the pictures on page 2."

I see a magnifying glass, a scale, a clock, a watering pail, a shovel, a tool kit, a toaster, a mixing machine, and an iron. I immediately pick out the clock, shovel, and toaster. This is easy.

"Great," Ashley says. "You got that one right away. Let's try another one."

I see an airplane, a bird, a boat, a train, a bicycle, and a car. There are a lot of choices on the next page: a wheelbarrow, a motorboat, a car, a truck, a train, a sailboat, a helicopter, and a bicycle. It takes me a while to sort through these images, and I say "Truck, sailboat, car."

Ashley shakes her head. "You missed a couple. Probably you got fooled because there are so many choices. Look at them again but slowly this time."

I stare at the pictures slowly, and really pay attention. This time, I see the bike, then the boat, and the train, although I have some doubt as to whether this is correct.

"You got it," Ashley encourages me. "Look at the next one."

This one has bananas, peppers, grapes, a watermelon slice, a basket of mushrooms, and a pumpkin. I turn the page and peruse the array, deciding to take my time and be careful not to let my thoughts wander.

"Bananas." I pause. There is no corn, or broccoli or lettuce, and no cantaloupes on the first page. The peppers look familiar but the pears do not. Then I identify the watermelon.

"Got it," I announce. "Watermelon slice, and a bunch of grapes."

When I give Ashley my list, she nods. "You were able to do that by taking your time. How did that feel?"

"Strenuous; running out of energy. Can we stop?"

"Yes, this is a good time to wrap up. You did well, because this one involves categories, memory, and word finding all at the same time. This was actually quite a hard exercise. A lot of speech therapy is not just getting words out of your mouth; it's also important to understand and exercise these skills."

We stand up, and as I gather up my coat and say goodbye, I think I will go home and watch some mindless TV.

STORIES

"Let's try some stories today," Ashley suggests. "But I need you to stop using telegraphic speech, which is condensing a sentence to the bare minimum. You may have used TS at an earlier stage so other people wouldn't hear how you were really speaking. I need to hear you so I know what to do for you."

"I will that do."

"You reversed 'that' and 'do,'" Ashley says. "Put them in the right order."

"I will do it."

Now she says, "Would you like to try reading stories and answering some questions about them?"

I can see that the worksheet is long and complicated.

Ashley reads aloud: "Jennifer and Jamie traveled by train to stay with their grandparents for the weekend. Their grandma and grandpa were delighted to have them visit and had planned several things to do on Saturday. First, they would go to the zoo, then to the children's favorite restaurant, and finally see a movie."

"Who went to the zoo?" Ashley asks.

"Jennifer, Jamie, grandma, and g-g-granddad."

"How did Jennifer and Jamie get to where they were going?" Ashley asks.

"They went by train," I reply.

"Were grandpa and grandma happy to see them?"

"Very much," I answer.

Ashley continues and asks what they had planned to do.

"Going to the zoo and then dinner." I pause. "At a restaurant." I pause again. "Um…then comes a movie."

"That's very good," Ashley exclaims. "You got all of that right. You understand all the concepts. You have a couple of syntax problems which have to do with putting words in the right order. We'll do another story and see if you can improve on that."

This one is longer and far more complicated.

"Mister Patterson was a carpenter who specialized in sailboat building. He loved his time with his family. He had developed a daily routine so he could have time for both his work and taking his wife and children out fishing in the boats he built. First, early in the morning, he would have a family breakfast and then go to work until four o'clock. In the evening he spent time on building his third boat before they all went fishing. Mrs. Peterson liked fishing, but she made her husband agree to clean any fish she brought home before she would cook them."

"Who was a carpenter?" Ashley inquires.

This time I think carefully about my answers. "Mr. Peterson he was a carpenter."

"Did he like spending time with his family?"

"Berry very much he does," I answer.

"What does he like to do?

"Wishing, dishing come fishing."

"When would he go fishing?"

"Into the evening."

"Did Mrs. Peterson like cleaning fish?"

"Not at all; she made him c-c-clean them before supper."

Ashley is pleased and tells me I did well. "You did have some stuttering, repeating words, and rhyming. I think we mainly need to work on your syntax and try not to rhyme things. Pause instead and wait for the right word to come. Sentence building might really help."

"What is that?"

"It helps you practice arranging the words to make complete and accurate sentences. I will start that that next time."

I am excited about doing something that sounds interesting. I leave with a feeling that I am about to take a big step.

BELMONT ABBEY

"I don't want to go tomorrow, after all," I tell Don.

"You mean speech therapy?" I nod. "Why not?" he asks.

"I'm fired, wired, tired, going three times a week, through intense exercises. Need a break."

"I think you should go," Don replies. "Ashley told you it's important to be consistent and not just give up unless you are not feeling well. Are you feeling OK?"

"Yes," I reply. "Maybe just need to do something different today way."

"Would you like to ride with me to the Abbey? It's a fine day for that."

"Sounds like fun, I would like to," I say.

We gather our things and set out on I-85; soon we see the towers and spires of the campus, where Don is Director of Library Services.

We take out my rollator and walk up to the library. Hannah is just inside the door on her way out.

"Nice to see you, Meredith. I haven't seen you in a long time and you look good today. Don says you're doing speech therapy now and I'm sure you're glad that's happening."

I nod and smile at her. "Yes, thank you."

Inside I see a display of medieval books, the Abbey being a Catholic college. Most of the displays have religious content. Don and most other faculty and staff don't have to be Catholic, but the sacred books are appealing, with vellum covers and pages bordered with bright colored inks. I am happy to sit looking them over while Don zips into his office to take care of some paperwork that has piled up in his absence.

"Would you like to go outside and see the garden?" he suggests when he comes back on out.

"Yes please, I haven't seen them this time of year," I let him know.

The trees are bare, the branches are the skeletons of the trees. The camellia bushes, cold weather plants, are a profusion of soft red and white blooms. It's pleasant to just sit still and look at them. The sky is blue with a few white clouds and a slight breeze blowing.

Placid Solari appears. He is the Abbot and is known for his contemplative walks.

He stops to greet us and asks me how my recovery is going.

"How are you doing? I hear that you were doing speech therapy now; is that helping?"

"It's helping," I answer.

"Would you like me to bless you?"

"Absolutely," I answer.

He prays in Latin, which I remember from high school.

"Thank you, Abbot."

We watch him walking away, his long robe flapping as he speeds up, but he turns around to wave goodbye.

I am getting tired but I am glad we came. The prayers and

blessings of an Abbot are certainly very special and they bring me relief from my difficulties.

SENTENCE BUILDING

Relaxed from our trip to Belmont Abbey, I enter Ashley's office looking forward to do sentence building. She greets me with a worksheet, which has unfamiliar open lines on it.

"Your speech has really been improving, so this is the right time for us to start sentence building. What are the two most important words in a sentence?" she asks.

"Noun and verb," I answer.

"And what do you think goes between those?"

I search my mind and come up with 'object.' Suddenly I guess what the open lines on her worksheet might be for.

"Exactly right," she smiles. "Look on the chart and write what words a person might use in an email."

"Why would he want to send an email?" I ask Ashley. "Just wondering!"

Ashley comments, "Let's try a prepositional phrase: 'He was travelling with some girls in his class.' The prepositions in this sentence are 'with' and 'in,' leading to the prepositional phrases 'with some girls' and 'in his class.' The first prepositional phrase modifies who she was traveling with, and then the second prepositional phrase modifies the previous one."

This is a functional sentence. Could I produce my own?

"Try making your own," Ashley suggests. She hands me another sheet and I give it a shot.

"A cat jumps onto the window-sill." Subject—verb—object. Then I wonder why the cat does that, and think about it for awhile. Then it comes to me.

"To watch birds," I say. "Flying birds. Adjective—noun."

A wave of happiness washes over me. This is easy.

She hands me half a dozen worksheets and says, "Work on these before next time and try making more complex sentences. You are really talking now!"

RUBY'S QUEST

Waking from a dream, I sense that is important and I must not let it slip away. I'm sure that it was about a dragon, and what else? Oh, the dragon was red and her name was Ruby.

Throughout the morning, things keep coming to me about this red dragon, such as her flying with a man in armor riding her and carrying a sword. But in my dream this dragon seems to be gentle, so what is she doing in a fight? I am sure she is not at heart a warrior, although I can't tell you why. What kind of dragon is Ruby?

These questions are couched in the format of sentence building, as if I need to arrange them in my mind element by element. By mid-morning I visualize her having an argument with her rider; his name is Prince Proud Head, and she is saying to him, "I don't want to fight anymore."

Words and images are crowding into my mind, and I go to my laptop to begin writing some of these down. Prince Proud Head had summoned a giant dragon, black and gold. His name is Blaze. The Prince leaps up on his back and yells "I've got a real dragon now!"

So what is Ruby going to do now? I don't know what to write

down yet. After lunch, more of the story comes to me. I sit down again and write about her crying, but that's not right.

After a while I realize that she wants to look for an alternative.

Where does she go? What does Ruby do next? What does she look like? I am still visualizing sentence-building worksheets. Noun: Ruby. Verb: to go. Object: the countryside. Adverb: how slowly. Yes, she sets off, wondering which direction to go. She chooses a path and moves ahead, her red tail dragging along green grass.

Now I am tired and lie down for a while, until more words arrive. Ruby believes there is a place that will make her happy. Suddenly she remembers the hatchery where she was born and decides to fly there. When she arrives she sees that eggs are hatching and that the mother dragons are swamped. Ruby lands and begins encouraging one of the baby dragons trying to peck its way out of its egg.

After dinner I don't still know what happens next. But at last I begin to see the rest of the story unfold. I build another sentence, and this seems as if Ruby begins writing the story herself.

The hatchlings need to learn how to walk and fly, and Ruby thinks "I'm here to teach them."

My eyes are getting fuzzy and I'm exhausted, dropping spoons all around, but I feel I must press on to the end. Ruby does what to whom and how and why, I say to myself as I build another sentence.

"Come on," she urges the young dragons, now beginning to fly. "I know you can do it!" They flap awkwardly but they are happy in the air. Ruby feels joyful and takes off flying herself.

Just a little bit more. Can I make it? Or will I run out of spoons? Ruby thinks that she now has a much better life and that maybe she will have an egg herself someday. Prince Proud Head and

Blaze were jerks. She doesn't need them. As she flies up into the blue sky she has a feeling of contentment she has never had before.

Where did these words come from? Clearly from sentence building, but it is as if my imagination has been set free.

NON-DUALISTIC EXPERIENCE

I'm sitting on the couch preparing to meditate. The tree in the back yard is surrounded by snow and its leaves and branches are swirling.

I wonder if I can project my spirit into this scene. Suddenly my eyes blur and merge into the tree as I become one with the dark branches. Time disappears.

The snow projects from the top of the tree to its roots. It is moving up and down. I lose myself. I am the tree and the tree is me.

This seems to go on outside time. What is this? Why is it happening to me? This is lovely and dynamic.

At last my consciousness is suspended and I see that the phenomenon is over, leaving me with a sense of bliss. I sit for some time looking at the white quietness.

I pick up my phone and call Pema to explain the experience. "What was this?" She pauses before responding.

"Meredith, you have had a non-dualistic experience."

"Do you mean the kind you have always been talking about?"

"Yes, this is wonderful. It's the kind of phenomenon which

comes along rarely and gives you an insight into the universe. How do you feel?"

"I feel my mind has opened up."

END OF SPEECH THERAPY

Ashley takes me to her desk which today is empty.

"No papers for me?" I ask.

"No. I think this is a good time for us to end. I'm going to give you the evaluation test again to make sure we've met all the goals of therapy."

This doesn't seem to be as long and difficult as the pretest had been. "You did well on this," she comments. "I hope you feel a sense of accomplishment."

"I really do, especially since this is around the one-year anniversary of my surgery."

She then shows me a picture of a dragon and says, "I showed your story to my kids last night and they were excited about it. It looks like you have turned a corner. What are you going to do with the story?"

"Try to publish it."

"It may take you a couple of tries, but it is a good project for you in terms of your new progress. That sentence building helps you take this therapy and try to do something new with it."

"Tell me what you think about the therapy that we did," I say to her.

"I think you may not get completely able to have a conversation right away, but at least I think you will be able to have discussions with your friends. Remember that you will still most likely have lapses. You have limitations now. These are things that you will just have to accept."

"Yes, you're right," I say, "Thanks for reminding me of that."

But I know I will always be trying to get even better.

EPILOGUE

THE JUGGLER

I stand on a crystal ball, feet above the ground and my head (encircled by metal bands), up in the stars. I am juggling. This image, which looks like a Tarot card, flashes in my mind quite suddenly, telling me how and where I am right now, what I am dealing with every day. In recent months I have become more impaired by multiple sclerosis, but my brain training remains intact.

My life has been radically altered; things will never be the same.

The most noticeable change is that I have to have regular MRI screenings to make sure the tumor has not come back or appeared in a new location. Astrocytoma can either return or set up shop in another part of the brain. I always have a moment of dread in the MRI machine, but it's important for me to remember that my tumor had a genetic mutation which made it especially vulnerable to Temodar, the chemotherapeutic agent used in my treatment.

The most important change, though, is that I have regained the ability to speak, to the point that I can have complex, meaningful conversations with other people. This is the best thing to come out of this, since communication has been key in my life. I recall my desperate striving to talk as a child, how I longed to be able to let my parents know what I was feeling. I've read that children don't remember that stage of life, but I do.

Fortunately I didn't have to start from square one during my struggle back from brain cancer, but I often revisit my childhood sense that the effort to communicate was the most difficult aspect of my life, and that it deserved all my attention.

There are changes in my brain which will not go away. I still pause in mid-sentence, fishing for the word I want to say. I still use the wrong word sometimes, substitute a rhyming word for what I want to say, transpose words, slur, and run words together. But these occur on a scale so much smaller now that, with a little care, I can express myself with far fewer errors. Nobody says "I don't know what you mean" anymore, and my writing has followed the same path.

My reading remains slow and laborious. I sometimes have to deconstruct sentences to make sure of the subject, verb and object, going back to re-read the sentence. Over time, focusing and paying extra attention, I am becoming more able to read at more complex adult levels, but I still like to relax my brain with books for younger readers, especially dragon stories, which capture my imagination. I have even written, in addition to Ruby's Quest, three more children's books about dragons. All the same, I will never be a fast reader.

Some people think that reading out loud can in some cases improve reading comprehension and speech. My oncologist encourages me to keep working on it. I have observed that when I read Spanish out loud I understand it better than when I read it silently. Speech, writing, and reading are functions of different loci in the temporal lobe, but the brain is a dynamic system.

My memory works better than it did earlier, but I am prone to forget things I've just been told and fail to follow through on tasks that I plan to do at a later time. If I set something down for a minute, I may be unable to remember where I put it; if something isn't in front of me, it doesn't exist. While, as so many brain patients say, I can remember something that happened when I was ten better than what happened this morning.

My base-level cognitive skills are lower than before the cancer. For example, our bowls are stored in the cabinet to the left of the sink and cups stored to the right. If I want a bowl, I will go to the cup cabinet and vice versa. Once I tried to put the dinner dishes in the refrigerator rather than in the dishwasher, which made us all laugh.

I'm left with the inability to handle numbers at all. I recognize some of the numbers that pop up on my phone screen, but I have had to write down my own phone number because when I try to give it to someone I transpose the numbers. Without a calculator, I couldn't add a couple of integers. While the temporal lobe handles words, my surgery touched on the border of the parietal, which governs numerical ability.

There is no such thing as full recovery from brain cancer, and for all the improvement, I sometimes feel that part of me is missing, that the removal of something from my brain has captured and taken from me some essential aspect of being and presence.

But the brain is so complex that we don't understand how it can contain what we call soul and spirit, how it can house our abilities to create, to love and be loved, and to desire connection with the universe, reaching out from within.

"Meredith," myself, is still here. Though I have striven with difficulty to speak, I can be heard. Being alive and conscious is a great and undeniable gift, one which not everyone with brain cancer has been given.

The greatest part of this gift is love. It was love which carried

227

me through this ordeal, and my greatest desire is to return that love.

June 21, 2021

Made in the USA
Columbia, SC
12 September 2021

44760004R00145